Question of German Unification

The Question of German Unification by Imanuel Geiss presents an introduction to the last two hundred years of German history and addresses questions raised by the status of Germany as a single or split national state. Updating his earlier work on the subject, Imanuel Geiss counters possible objections from both the Left and Right.

Events in Eastern Europe, the collapse of European Communism and German reunification have once again brought issues of Germany's status into the arena of world politics. Imanuel Geiss argues that Germany has fluctuated all too frequently, and catastrophically, between the status of power centre in Europe and power vacuum. *The Question of German Unification* focuses on special features of German history and looks at Germany within a European framework. By detailing long-term structures and processes, the author analyses the political, economic and social aspects of German nationalism as well as the impact on Germany of the collapse of Communism.

The Question of German Unification includes discussion of recent political events as well as a chronology and further reading. Imanuel Geiss reflects on the irrationalities of German history, surveys how they have been explained by historians, and provides a succinct and readable account of the complex issues.

Imanuel Geiss is Emeritus Professor of history at Bremen University. His publications include *8 July 1914*, *The Pan-African Movement*, *Geschichte griffbereit*, *Geschichte im Überblick*, *Europa – Einheit und Vielfalt*, *Der Jugoslawienkrieg*, *Geschichte des Rassismus* and *Der Zerfall der Sowjetunion*.

Fred Bridgham is the author of studies of Rilke, Kafka and Nietzsche, and of other essays on German history and culture. His most recent book is *The Friendly German–English Dictionary* (Libris, 1996). He ...nslated Hans Werner Henze's *Der Prinz von Homburg* for perform-... by English National Opera.

The Question of German Unification

1806–1996

Imanuel Geiss

Translated by
Fred Bridgham

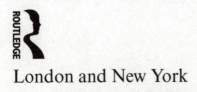

London and New York

First published in 1997 in this translation
by Routledge
11 New Fetter Lane, London EC4P 4EE

Simultaneously published in the USA and Canada
by Routledge
29 West 35th Street, New York, NY 10001

Translated from the German: *Die deutsche Frage 1806–1990*,
© Bibliographisches Institut & F.A. Brockhaus AG, Mannheim 1992.
This translation © 1997 Routledge

Typeset in Times by RefineCatch Limited, Bungay, Suffolk

Printed and bound in Great Britain by
Clays Ltd, St. Ives PLC

British Library Cataloguing in Publication Data
A catalogue record for this book is available from the British Library

Library of Congress Cataloguing in Publication Data
Geiss, Imanuel.
    [Deutsche Frage. English]
    The question of German unification: 1806–1996 / Imanuel Geiss.
       p.   cm.
    Includes bibliographical references.
    1. German reunification question (1949–1990) 2. Nationalism–
Germany–History. 3. Germany–History–1789–1900. 4. Germany–
History–20th century. 5. Germany–Relations–Europe. 6. Europe–
Relations–Germany. I. Title.
DD203.G4513   1997

943′.07–dc21   96–52536

ISBN 0–415–15049–3

Contents

Preface

Interest in 'the German Question' increased throughout the 1980s both in the Federal Republic and in the former GDR – if only in a subdued way in the East, where public opinion inevitably remained underground and unarticulated. With the collapse of European communism in 1989/91, the German Question re-entered the agenda of world politics. Since then, the need for a full account of its special features and peculiarities has become ever more pressing. Germany has oscillated all too often, and catastrophically, between being either a power centre or a power vacuum in Europe. But an attempt to explain the German Question in these terms should not be thought of as reflecting some new consciousness of German power. It is entirely pragmatic. Within a necessarily brief compass, it is the political dimension which most readily permits a clear reading of German history, though one also naturally grounded in economic and social history, and embedded at least briefly in a European framework.

I am grateful to the publishers for the opportunity to produce this long-planned, compact overview, an elaboration on several preliminary studies. For reasons of space, and since a similar volume on European history has already appeared,[1] I have concentrated on the German Question in the period between 1806 and 1990, merely sketching in earlier developments.[2] My approach has been a macro-historical one: understanding long-term structures and processes is more important than an accumulation of undigested details. For the orientation of interested readers, a chronological table at the end supplies the relevant sequence of dates. Hence, this is *not* a pocket German history, but an essay trying to explain, in a systematic and roughly chronological way, the volatile recent course of German history. In the notes, which have been kept to a minimum, I acknowledge ideas for which I am indebted to other authors or where more detailed treatment of problems by the present author is to be found: the more generally known a subject, such as the First or Second World Wars, the Holocaust or the Cold War, the more superfluous and indeed unhelpful bibliographical references become.

My thanks to Frau Renate Brock and Frau Gabriele Intermann of Bremen for providing a fair copy and for their critical and constructive help at the manuscript stage.

Imanuel Geiss
Bremen, March 1992

Introduction to English edition

This slightly expanded English edition retains the tight overall structure rigorously imposed by the original format – to the ultimate benefit, it is to be hoped, of the book itself. At the same time, released from the German strait-jacket, it provides an opportunity to answer criticisms and anticipate possible objections, both hostile and legitimate: it does not aim to provide a comprehensive survey of German history in the nineteenth and twentieth centuries, but rather a succinct and readable account of the bewilderingly complex issues raised by what is loosely known as 'the German Question'. Historians of the progressive Left also speak of Germany's 'special path' as something which distinguishes her from 'the West', though without attempting to define these terms in a rational – that is to say, an historical – way.

Faced with the irrationalities of German history, German historians have themselves reflected only too faithfully its sudden discontinuities and disastrous swings from one extreme to the other. Until 1968, a year of symbolic significance, the 'German hysteria'[1] was to be found mainly on the Right. Since then, the Left has taken up Fritz Fischer's critique of the national myths and legends of German history concerning the First World War,[2] but in the process has overstated and distorted his valuable and accurate insights, culminating in the so-called *Historikerstreit* (1986/7) with its denunciations of even a rational, moderate line as 'nationalistic' and 'right-wing'.[3] In its anti-anti-communist hysteria, the new orthodoxy of the Left, represented above all by Jürgen Habermas and Hans-Ulrich Wehler, remained blind to the agony and final death throes of Soviet communism, clearly visible to others since the war in Afghanistan[4]. After the collapse of communism in 1989/91, some elements of the Left have begun to adopt the very positions formerly denounced. Where it was once inadmissible to compare communism and National Socialism as twin paradigms of totalitarianism,[5] for instance, since this allegedly trivialized the crimes of German Nazism, now the parallel is made quite blatantly in a way which, before 1989/91, would have been condemned by the Left as an apologia for National Socialism, and which in the *Historikerstreit* would have been labelled neo-conservative.

Consequently, the leading German historians have as yet been unable to provide a coherent and convincing historical explanation for the collapse of Communism and its impact on Germany. Since criticism of the present attempt at orientation is to be expected from adherents of the Habermas-Wehler school, some introductory remarks are necessary; reasons of space alone prevented their inclusion in the German edition. In Germany, this first attempt, however inadequate, to give an historical explanation for the events of 1989 has met with total silence from the 'honest scholarship' of the new orthodoxy of the Left, whose leader (Wehler) duly passed verdict on the author by letter as an 'intolerable renegade'. Critical discussion – long overdue, yet something which ought to go without saying in a scholarly and democratic context – might now perhaps be set in motion in Germany via the English-speaking world.

Essentially, the structure of the book remains unaltered: it looks at fluctuations in Germany's fortunes between its status as a power vacuum since the late Middle Ages, and the three occasions – 1871, 1938, 1990 – when it rose to become a power centre. Since experience suggests that 'power vacuum' and 'power centre' may not be totally self-explanatory to English readers, the introductory section offers some brief elucidation of these elementary categories in relation to Germany past and present, and of two further key concepts in the history of power: 'quantitative' and 'qualitative'.

Speculation as to what might or could have happened differently in German history since 1806 seems fruitless: alleged or real alternatives either dissolve of their own accord, or else, as so often in history, they manifest themselves in a roundabout way and in modified circumstances, in which case they will be duly dealt with. There are so many real historical facts, structures and processes to analyse that it would be simply a waste of time and space to labour over such sterile fictions as 'the invention of the nation', itself a recent invention of historians which takes apart the key concept of the 'nation' but is unable to offer any explanation of its real explosive force – not just in Germany. It is more important to illuminate the logic of the real historical processes of the *longue durée* (F. Braudel) as it applies to Germany, than to split hairs over the relation of politically influential élites and the 'public opinion' they shape to the mainly anonymous 'masses' who, for the most part, ultimately follow their élites – both those who control opinion and (except in transitional, revolutionary situations) those who rule over them.

In order to highlight the European dimension, two short sections have been added to the introductory chapter. One of these deals with Germany's place in the architecture of Europe, 'Germany' here signifying all areas with German-speakers within distinctively 'German' states, irrespective of their power-political complexion – whether German 'Reich' (First, Second, Third), German Confederation, or Republic (First, Second) – within internationally recognized boundaries, fluctuate as these may in the wake of various conflicts. The second section expands an existing paragraph on other national questions since the French Revolution, in order to bring out more clearly what distinguishes the German national question. In addition, the sub-chapter on 'Germany's special path' has been extended. The Weimar Republic and the Third Reich up to the outbreak of the Second World War have now been given a sub-chapter each and sketched more fully. The final chapter, covering the period since reunification, has been modified and brought up to date, as has the chronological table. Several titles have been added to the bibliography, especially works in English. On the other hand, some details deemed too technical for English readers have been omitted.

Imanuel Geiss
Bremen, April 1997

1 Conceptual and European framework

German history is too important to be left to the Germans alone. They cultivate national introspection, the Right stressing the primacy of foreign policy (*Primat der Außenpolitik*), and the Left the primacy of domestic affairs (*Primat der Innenpolitik*). As yet, no rational definition of the German Question has been given in the broader European context. Germany's 'special path' (*Sonderweg*), recently conjured up by those on the Left, only makes sense as a German variant of other nations' 'special paths' or 'national questions'. Since the complementary notions of power vacuum – power centre and quantity – quality are universal ones, their application to the German Question promises a greater degree of objectivity.

CONCEPTUAL FRAMEWORK: POWER

National questions such as the German Question are invariably connected with the political organization of peoples into states of varying size, and with their status as a power vacuum or a power centre. Thence, a general definition of power is called for.

Quality and quantity

The German word for power, *Macht*, comes from the Indo-European **maghd*. It suggests that one is 'able to do something', for instance, to raise one's standard of living, to 'lead the good life' (Aristotle). The word signifies a combination of people with economic potential (= capability) and social organization, leading to centralization and hierarchical military structures – armies, navies – under a strong ruler. Consequently, power only develops world-historical importance with the advent of civilization in city-states and empires, first in Mesopotamia and Egypt around 3,000 BC. This is why, for Aristotle, the state only comes into existence as the institutionalized embodiment of power when it replaces random scatterings of individual dwellings and villages. Nomads, too, only developed power by forming concentrated military structures.

'Quantity' and 'quality' – concepts ideally suited to a nuanced analysis of power and state – are also to be found in Aristotle's *Politics*, but appear to have been forgotten by modern historians and political scientists in their analysis of power: 'We have to remember that quality and quantity both go to the making of every state. By "quality" we mean free birth, wealth, culture and nobility of birth; by "quantity" we mean superiority in numbers.'[1]

Nowadays, to size of population one would add to the definition of quality the size of territory, analysed by Aristotle as well: it is either roughly proportional to the size of population or else can itself become a strategic or security factor by virtue of its sheer extent – the size of Russia or China, for instance, as a protection against foreign invasions. Conversely, great territorial size can become a heavy burden and make a country ungovernable – witness the break-up of the Soviet Union and pressures within post-Soviet Russia.[2]

Naturally, size of population requires further classification: ethnic, linguistic, cultural and/or religious homogeneity or heterogeneity are important factors, as is the distinction between the core population of a state and its subject or dependent peoples, usually more towards the peripheries. For power structures of whatever size, the basic rule of thumb is generally a fifty-fifty relationship.

When determining 'quality', Aristotle still provides the key, though with his categories perhaps requiring slight modification: it is no accident that 'freedom' comes first – the innate sense of qualitative superiority which the classical citizen of the *polis* felt towards all 'barbarians'. 'Aristocracy' translates into today's 'ruling élite' or 'political class'; 'wealth' becomes 'economic strength', as expressed by the gross national products of modern states. 'Education' remains as then, now and for the foreseeable future, a key factor.

Today's historians have a great deal more illustrative material than Aristotle did over 2,000 years ago: with literally countless examples of the 'quantity' and 'quality' of states, both past and present, to draw on, we can go beyond Aristotle and correlate 'quantity' with 'quality' by adapting Einstein's famous formula $E = mc^2$ – though in a symbolical sense, of course, rather than a strictly mathematical one: Power = Quantity × Quality^2.

The greater weighting of quality over quantity explains the often stupendous world-historical effect of small peoples living in small territories (e.g. Portugal, Holland), of city states (Sumerian, Phoenician, Greek), or of the Jews, but also the combined effect of quantity and quality on a large scale (China). Conversely, the formula explains why quantitative strength may turn to weakness when qualititative factors are underdeveloped or have had a dysfunctional, self-destructive effect, as in Russia.

Power vacuum – power centre

A power vacuum is a region without a central government and army. It arises not through the partial or complete absence of power, but when fragmented groups of varying size and strength neutralize each other through mutual rivalry and are rendered incapable of external action, especially of common defence or aggression. In a power vacuum the tendency is towards anarchy or chaos – from primal chaos on the level of pre-agrarian family groupings (hunters and gatherers) and extensive agrarian producers (farmers, nomads) in tribal structures, up to tribal kingdoms and confederations. Secondary chaos in power vacuums generally appears after the dissolution of an imperial superstructure such as an empire and its successor states.

Power vacuums sooner or later attract intervention and conquest by culturally more advanced or militarily stronger power centres. Secondary power vacuums often become the battleground for surrounding major powers, until one of the participants in the internal power struggle for hegemony is successful and establishes a new power centre. States in internal turmoil – as a result of revolution or civil war – temporarily become power vacuums, until such time as order is re-established.

Examples of power centres of varying size and duration, on the other hand, are regions with a central government and army, which often have some of their forces stationed outside their own borders, which is also where they prefer to wage their wars.

The history of states and of power finds spectacular expression in the cyclical rise and fall of power centres and their subsequent collapse into power vacuums. Economic and social history is closely linked in such processes, since it is a country's economy and social structures which constitute power in the first place. All power centres sooner or later expand by conquest; in modern times also overseas. Generally, some serious military defeat on the periphery provokes internal crisis – in modern times, revolutions and decline of power or an outright collapse.[3]

Power in relation to the German Question

Like all peoples or regions, the Germans, too, have fluctuated through-out their history between the status of power vacuum and that of power centre. After a diffuse pre-history, German history began with the polit-ical union of the *Regnum Teutonicum* in 911. Against a background of feudal fragmentation during the centuries of chaos after the fall of the Western Roman Empire, the German kingdom suddenly emerged, almost from nowhere at the fringes of Latin Europe, as the first power centre in medieval Europe. In 1198 a battle for the German throne between the Staufen and the Guelphs precipitated a centuries-long decline into a power vacuum which lasted until the founding of the Second Reich in 1871. As a continental superpower, the Second Ger-man Reich then pursued the *fata Morgana* of European hegemony and ascent to world-power status, with catastrophic results: the First World War (whence the Germans failed to draw the lesson that it was impos-sible to defeat the proverbial 'world of enemies'), National Socialism, Third Reich, Second World War, the division of Germany as part of the division of the world along ideological and power-political lines. German reunification in 1990 came about only in the wake of the Soviet débâcle.

Strictly speaking, the German Question existed in a formal sense only during two periods when the Germans had no single national state: from 1806 to 1871, and from 1945 to 1990. But uniting the Germans in a single state was a uniquely explosive issue, and its coroll-ary becomes inescapable: *how* would the Germans use such power as they achieved simply by uniting? Like all other new power centres, they sooner or later embarked collectively on the power-political road to expansion, thus the architecture of the European system must provide an answer to the question of why German expansion destroyed the European system itself, in two world wars.

The explosive nature of German unity can also be attributed to the specific rapport between quantity and quality, whence the power of a united Germany: quantitatively, in terms of population and territory, the Germans were always number two in Europe, behind the French until around 1850 and then behind Russia. In addition, isolated terri-tories inhabited by Germans extended throughout eastern and south-eastern Europe, forming far-flung pockets of German minorities. Every claim to unite *all* Germans in a single Reich – as raised by the Pan-Germans after 1890 – thereby inflated the territory claimed by Germans to the point of becoming self-defeating. Furthermore, some of the major German states contained areas in which, to a greater (Austria) or lesser (Prussia) extent, Germans constituted a minority – at best a dominant political, social, economic or cultural minority. Inevitably, they clashed with non-German majorities during the era of awakening national movements.

Qualitatively, Germany in the Middle Ages occupied a roughly central position in Latin Europe, between the most important economic and cultural centres in the South (Italy) and West (France) which had been civilized in varying degrees by Roman tradition passed down a thousand years before, and the North (Scandinavia), which had remained barbarous for much longer, together with the East. It was precisely this central position which made Germany, right down to modern times, the great link between western influences from Italy (church, local autonomy, culture in the broadest sense of the word) and France (medieval land development and the arts) and the rest of Europe.

As a power vacuum, 'Germany' had been little more than a geographical concept. But its cultural rise, followed by its economic recovery after the Thirty Years War, and especially the explosion of classical culture around 1800 while it was still politically fragmented and powerless, gave it such momentum that industrialization after *c*.1850 progressively pushed it qualitatively into a leading position. Its traditional quantitative strength combined with this modern qualitative strength to facilitate its abrupt emergence as the strongest power on the continent, even without the Austrian Germans. In spite of two defeats, in 1918 and 1945 – the second even worse than the first – the divided Germany of the Cold War remained potentially an important power both quantitatively and qualitatively, though in many respects the two Germanies tended to neutralize each other.

THE EUROPEAN FRAMEWORK

In addition to the German dimension of such universal factors as quantity and quality, there are specifically German aspects of the European system, some of which are examined below.

The architecture of the European system

Europe is a complex system of varying entities – peoples, states, regions. Compared with other subcontinental units of similar size, such as China and India, it is distinguished by a different combination of unity and diversity. China is the centralized, all-assimilating, unitary megastate *par excellence*. It was no accident, according to de Tocqueville, that oppositional intellectuals (*philosophes*) at the end of the *ancien régime* saw it as their ideal state. India, on the other hand, with its social base of family, caste and village, for much of its history has experienced chronic chaos as states fragmented, their size and character changing continuously, with only a few periods of imperial unity. The British raj was the longest period of subcontinental unity for India. Politically, China and India were held together during the last millenium by their respective imperial capitals in the north, Beijing (Peking) and Delhi.

Europe, by contrast, was never a united empire – certainly not after the fall of the Western Roman Empire in 476. Out of feudal chaos there finally emerged, through prolonged conflict, a pentarchy of European powers between the Congress of Vienna in 1815 and the outbreak of the First World War in 1914. Since then, the European system has become fragmented through the advent of new national states, above all after the First World War when there emerged successor states of the four great dynastic empires – Czarist Russia in 1917, Austria-Hungary and Germany in 1918 and the Ottoman Empire in 1920/24 – and again with the post-Communist successor states after the collapse of the Soviet Union and Yugoslavia in 1989/91.

Instead of imperial unity on the continent, there was always an anti-hegemonic, even an anti-imperial, impulse behind its pluralistic system: whichever of the European powers has attempted to gain sole dominion over Europe has been put in its place by Grand Alliances: France (twice), Russia in the Crimean War, Germany (twice). Since Europe has never constituted a single empire, it has never had a continental capital such as Beijing or Delhi.

While lacking a continental imperial capital, Europe nevertheless has always had a centre: the Germans. If we think of the architecture of the European system as a complex arched Gothic vault, with further arches branching out since the political earthquake of 1989/91, then the Germans would be the capstone. However, given the Germans' quantitative and qualitative strength, this capstone is too heavy, it threatens to pull down the whole vault. The German capstone would function best in the European vault (and here the metaphor is no longer apt) if it were itself split to ease inner-European tensions. But the capstone must not crumble too much, or it will no longer function effectively.

The quantitative and the qualitative power of the united Germans is a burden both to Germany itself and to Europe. It demands of the Germans, in the centre of Europe, a dangerous balancing act between foregoing the imperial-cum-hegemonic consequences of their national unity, and accepting a low profile, if wanted.

Europe's internal structural boundaries

One reason for European plurality is the four great structural boundaries which criss-cross the continent.[4] These came into being where the various versions of civilization which have shaped Europe either stopped their forward march for, in each case, some three to four centuries (the Roman *limes*; the eastern and southern boundary of the Carolingian Empire), or else drew a fundamental divide through European civilization (Latin/Orthodox, 395/1054; Reformation/Counter-Reformation, 1517/63)

1 The boundaries of the Roman Empire, secured to the north and east by the *limes*, divided the civilized South and (since Caesar) West – the Iberian peninsula, Gaul, Roman Britain – from the still barbarous East and North, which were to remain barbarous for many centuries to come. What later became Germany is the only European country to straddle this boundary. This helps account for the later fluctuations and uncertainties which the Germans experienced with regard to their place in Europe. The Roman *limes* was accordingly the first internal structural boundary in Europe.

2 The final division of the Roman Empire saw civilized Europe disintegrate into a Latin West and a Greek East/South-East. Competing Christian missionary efforts from Rome and Constantinople extended the dividing line of 395 northward as far as Finland; religious confirmation of the division between Latin West and Orthodox East came with the schism of 1054. Each side developed in quite different ways, both outwardly and inwardly: in the West, individual freedom, the rule of law, and parliamentary democracy in modern nation states; in the East and South-East, autocratic power structures under the imperial control of despotic rulers.

3 Chronologically between the key dates 395 and 1054, and geographically between the *limes* and Latin/Orthodox divide, lies the structural boundary of 800: it is marked by the boundaries of the Carolingian Empire, especially with the then still pagan Slav East, and with southern Italy, conquered by the Muslims. True, the Italian Reconquista of 1030–90 and German colonization of the East beginning in 1137 outwardly removed the boundary of 800. But it continued as an inner-European structural boundary because the inhabitants of the reconquered areas in the south of Italy, and of those western parts of the Slav East conquered for the first time, then Christianized and largely Germanized, became all but second-class citizens on Reconquista or colonial soil. To the east of the Elbe, structural differences were renewed and deepened by the

'second serfdom' after 1492/98, when agrarian laws over the following centuries reduced peasants to serfs, and in Russia effectively to agrarian slaves. It is no accident that this boundary with the East of 800 and 1492/98 became the great world-structural divide of 1945, and remained so up to the collapse of communism.

4　The final structural boundary, unlike the others, divided the continent north–south, and in a double sense: At the end of the Reformation (from 1517) and the Counter-Reformation (from 1563), the North became predominantly Protestant, with characteristic variants (Lutheran, Calvinist, Anglican) and two exceptions: Ireland in the north-west, and Poland and Lithuania in the north-east, clinging staunchly to Catholicism. The South remained predominantly Catholic. The situation in the middle was mixed: Germany reproduced this pattern on a smaller scale – the North predominantly Protestant, the South predominantly Catholic, the middle mixed – and it is here that two of Europe's great religious wars were sparked off: the Schmalkaldan War of 1546/47 and the Thirty Years War of 1618–48.

Of these four internal structural boundaries, three run through Germany and consequently contributed to Germany's instability and fragmentation. The complexities of Europe account also for the bewildering oscillations of the Germans in their marginal position between East and West: culturally and politically, Germany belonged undoubtedly to the West, but following 1492/98 the eastern German areas began to slip towards the East in socio-economic terms. With the rise of Russia as the dominant hegemonic power in Eastern Europe, Germany increasingly drifted into the orbit of Russian autocracy, politically, torn and finally divided between East and West, 1945–90.

Zones of European nationality

After the Roman Empire reached the limits of its expansion on the *limes*, the peoples of Europe developed their statehood in quite different ways. It was on the territory of the Western Roman Empire that Germanic, post-Roman successor states first developed the earliest forms of proto-national monarchy, which was to become such an influential and distinctively European phenomenon, leading to the national monarchies of the high Middle Ages in Portugal, Spain, France and England. In both quantitative and qualitative terms, France was the most powerful kingdom and proto-national state, and following the French victory over England at Bouvines in 1214, the first and for a long time the only European great power. Both France and England flourished on what was to be the typically European combination of individual rights and politically representative bodies known as the Estates. In England, victory in the two revolutions (1640–60, 1688/89) achieved sovereignty of Parliament over the Crown; the later French Revolution produced a more modern and radical variant of the same principle – sovereignty of the people in a parliamentary republic.

The zone of undisputed national monarchies was joined after 1000 by the Scandinavian monarchies, and after 1291 by Switzerland as a confederation of sovereign cantons, and the new Low Countries, the States General – both national states of a new kind.

To the east and south of these national states were zones in which nationhood could be achieved only through radical change and upheaval. Several sub-zones can be discerned: first of all, peoples shaped by Latin influence, whether they were still Catholic or had become mainly Protestant.

Closest to the political West lay Italy and Germany, both (as post-Roman power vacuums) mere 'geographical concepts' without over-arching national statehood. Their problem became how to achieve a single-nation statehood according to the French model, to replace their fragmented political status. After 1815, the Italian Risorgimento and the founding of the German Reich were the answers to the Italian and German questions.

Further to the East, but still within the sphere of Latin influence, were peoples who had lost their own sovereign or autonomous statehood through incorporation into powerful imperial complexes: Croatia to Hungary (1102); Hungary through the catastrophe of Mohács in 1526 (and up to 1683), Bohemia to the Habsburgs at the beginning of the Thirty Years War after the catastrophe of the White Mountain (1620/23); and Poland through its three partitions to Russia, Prussia, Austria (1772, 1793, 1795). Other peoples had never had a state of their own (the Slovenes, Latvians and Estonians), or in the case of Finland, had fluctuated between Sweden and Russia, yet preserving their own autonomy. Further to the east and south-east, smaller peoples, Orthodox and part Slav, had lost their own proto-national state (the Serbs and Bulgars to the Ottoman Turks), or had never had one (the Albanians, Greeks and Ukrainians), while the Romanians occupied a special position. In the West, Basques and Irish suffered comparable fates.

National questions and 'special paths' (*Sonderwege*)

After the French and, later, Industrial Revolutions, all the peoples to the east of France and south of Scandinavia raised 'national questions'. In each case, the 'question' has to be taken literally: should People X, Y, Z obtain a state of their own? If so, within what boundaries, at what level of statehood (autonomous or sovereign), with what internal structure (federal, or unitary and centralized), by what methods (peaceful or through war)? The most important national questions arose in the following chronological order, usually after their loss of national sovereignty: Polish (1795), Irish (1800/01), South Slav (1804), German (1806), Italian (1815), Greek (1821), Belgian (1830), Hungarian (1848) and Jewish (as a reaction to pogroms in Russia, 1881).

In a formal sense, a national question was answered once a national movement had achieved its own state. But since nations after 1789 usually began as small states, they were as a rule dissatisfied with their original state boundaries. Thus, national questions have tended to smoulder on: South Slav up to the most recent war in former Yugoslavia,[5] Greek in chronic conflict with Turkey, Jewish in conflict with Middle Eastern neighbours over boundaries never yet set by themselves, and so on.

National questions, each with their different answer, in turn throw up the question of 'national special paths'. Large regions such as Europe, India, China, Black Africa, the Islamic Middle East, South-East Asia, etc. also have their own individual 'special paths', whether we define these as continental or subcontinental. Within these large-scale special paths there are as many 'national' special paths with regional or even local sub-variants as there are nation states, whether federally subdivided or not.

If 'special path' is not to degenerate into an irrational category – in Germany during the last few years, a self-accusatory and self-defeating one – then some general definition which adequately reflects modern complexities, is indispensable. 'Special paths' are the product of general factors (universal, European, Indian, Black African, etc.) of varying complexity and common to all, either in a global context or within a large region. They are also the product of two types of peculiarity – absolute exceptions which only apply to People X, Y or Z; and extreme positions in a whole spectrum of possibilities between extreme poles. In any equation which does even approximate justice to complex realities, there will be common denominators below the line and differentiating numerators above. In addition, all factors can change in time – increase or decrease[6].

'Reich' and 'Nation': modern nationalisms

Modern nationalisms claiming their own (autonomous or sovereign) statehood introduce a highly charged complication into national questions, since they appeal to historical precedents (usually 'empires' at the height of their power) in determining the boundaries of their new state. Inevitably, every imperial or sub-imperial definition of a 'national state' – 'Pan-Croatian', 'Pan-Bulgarian', 'Pan-Serbian', 'Pan-Hungarian', 'Pan-Romanian', 'Pan-German' etc. – provokes major external and internal conflicts. There are several reasons for this.

Empires are never homogeneous, but by definition heterogeneous. Since neighbouring peoples experienced the zenith of their former 'empires' at different times, areas to which they aspire overlap with areas to which others lay claim for 'historical' reasons. The conflicts between Croatia and Serbia over Bosnia-Herzegovina, or between Serbia, Bulgaria and Greece over Macedonia, are contemporary examples. Where 'historical' claims to heterogeneous areas containing perhaps only a small minority of a state's own 'nationals' are not sufficient, religious, economic or strategic 'reasons' are enlisted for further territorial aggrandizement.

Historically grounded 'empire' nationalism *vis-à-vis* the outside world soon brings in its wake one dire internal consequence, when the new centralizing nation-state aims at assimilation along the lines of the French revolutionary slogan, *la nation une et indivisible*. It escalates into repressive homogenization of those national minorities outside the neo-imperial titular 'nation', and abuse of individual and collective human rights. A neo-imperial definition of modern nationalisms and the 'imperative of the homogeneous nation' (K.H. Weissmann) are together the kiss of death for any modern national state, for they give rise to 'ethnic cleansing', to massacres and genocide, as seen recently in the war in Yugoslavia and in Russia's war with the Chechens.

SPECIFIC CHARACTERISTICS OF THE GERMAN QUESTION

Germany lies on the western border of those areas where 'national questions' erupted after 1789. With the exception of the Irish Question, all other national questions are dialectically linked with the German Question – mostly via Austria: positive answers to the Polish, South Slav, Italian, etc. Questions would always be at the expense of German power, in conflict with German states, both before and after the foundation of the Second Reich in 1871. General definitions of other national questions make it easier to define the German Question. Should the

Germans have a national state? If so, within what boundaries, with what internal structures, and by what methods? In the German case, additional issues are: with what consequences for themselves and for Europe? What will be the power-political status in Europe of a totally, or almost totally, united Germany?

Germany's central position in Europe

Germany's position as the central capstone of the European system has long had explosive consequences. With the creation of the new Reich of 1871, of all five Great Powers in the original European pentarchy, only Germany bordered on all of the other four (on Great Britain via the North Sea). If it wished to expand, as all new power centres do, it could do so only at the expense of one or other of these Great Powers. What German imperial chauvinism later demonized as 'encirclement' was thus already in place as one of the basic factors which made for the First World War.

Definition of the German Question

The German Question first appeared in 1806 when the Holy Roman Empire formally came to an end: what sort of political organization were the Germans to have in its place? One early reaction was Ernst Moritz Arndt's famous poem beginning: 'What is the Germans' Fatherland?' After listing various territories, again in the form of questions ('Is it the Prussian lands, is it the Bavarian lands?' etc.), there followed the equally famous answer: 'Let it be all of Germany!', and 'As far as the German tongue is heard'.

This addressed the crux of the matter, albeit poetically rather than in a systematic, rational way. After the dissolution of the old amorphous Reich, Arndt simply clothed the now urgent German Question in the guise of a question as to the German fatherland – a rather clumsy, old-fashioned synonym for 'nation', itself a term every bit as difficult to define. For de Gaulle, '*l'Europe des patries*' was a 'Europe of the nations', and 'nation' was essentially also what Gustav Heinemann (Federal President, 1969–74) meant by his memorable phrase 'Germany, a difficult fatherland'.

So the German Question is also a question as to the national identity of the Germans. It is no chauvinism to try to answer it in a constructive, positive way, for it is self-evident that every nation has an identity revealed by its history. The fact that the Germans have difficulties with their national identity, especially in connection with the Third Reich, the Second World War and Auschwitz, does not mean that they do not have a national identity.

A glance at other national questions makes it easier to see this in a European context. Older nation states – Portugal, Spain, France, England, Switzerland, 'Holland', Denmark and Sweden – have no 'national question'. Their identity and existence have never been seriously challenged, however much their form and substance changed over the centuries. But some European nations went through phases in which they had no state of their own, or else, like the Germans and Italians, had too many of them.

The German Question can also be put in the following way: how are the Germans to be organized in such a way that both they and their neighbours are equally satisfied at the same time? As yet, no such harmonious arrangement has ever been found. Historically, the search for it has seemed like trying to square the circle. All attempts depended on who provided the terms of the answer – foreign powers or a united Germany. Tension between German readiness to accept any given answer to the German Question, and their neighbours' response, has had its own explosive dynamic, culminating in two world wars.

Consequently, the notorious German Question appeared to be answered when the German national state came into being. From this perspective, the question was in abeyance between 1871 and 1945, but in reality it merely assumed new dimensions. For the logic of the geographical spread of Germans over central Europe gave rise to at least two variants of German national statehood: the *großdeutsch*, or Greater German alternative, including Austria (and originally also under Austrian leadership), and the *kleindeutsch*, or Lesser German alternative, under Prussian leadership, excluding Austria.

Germany's 'special path' as the sum of peculiarly German features

'Germany's special path' might be used to describe the particular path taken by Germany within the history of modern Europe, were it not for the fact that the term has recently come to be used in a more narrowly dogmatic and moralizing sense, confined to the historical circumstances which led to the rise of National Socialism and its two global crimes, the Second World War and the Holocaust. The general definition (sum of absolute exceptions and extreme positions) and a preliminary sketch of the main factors determining Germany's special position in Europe facilitate a systematic explanation[7]:

  1 Of all the peoples in Europe with unresolved national questions, the

Germans have always been the strongest, both in terms of quantity and quality.

2 After their great cultural flowering, symbolized by Viennese Classicism and Goethe's Weimar around 1800, the Germans rose throughout the nineteenth century to become the dominant European nation.

3 By virtue of their position at the geographical and power-political centre of Europe, the Germans – including the Austrians up to 1866 – had more neighbours than any other people in the world, a fact due in part to Europe's structural diversity. Only the Irish, Spaniards, Portuguese, Bulgarians and Greeks did not directly border on German states. Every other European people did, either directly by land, or by sea (Great Britain, Scotland, Norway, Finland, Sweden). The more neighbours, the more opportunity for friction and conflict, especially at times of German strength and power, since most of Germany's neighbours were in comparison small and correspondingly weak.

4 A further peculiarity was the logical sequel to Germany's central European location where the continent's major cultural regions meet – South and West, East and North, Germany straddling all of them. As long ago as Roman times, civilization and prosperity decreased the further north and the further east one went. Each of these gradients bisected Germany, creating inevitable tensions. In modern times, however, notably in the wake of the Industrial Revolution, the south–north gradient turned into a north–south gradient, extending on a global scale into Black Africa. But there was no such inversion of the west–east gradient, which has remained a constant of European history – more so than ever after the collapse of communism.

5 Since the Middle Ages, crucial innovations have been transmitted through Germany to the North and East – Roman Christianity even before 1000, medieval land development (the most intensive form of agrarian production at the time) from the west (the Paris basin), town and city councils from the south (Italy) after 1000. In addition, from the Rammelsberg near Goslar in the Harz Mountains, for centuries the most important silver mine in Europe, mining fanned out from Sweden to Bosnia. In modern times, as the centre of the Reformation, Germany had a powerful effect above all on northern and parts of eastern Europe; later, it was a conduit of industrialization from north-west Europe (Great Britain and Belgium). With the end of the Cold War, it is again centrally located, between the democratic West and the post-communist East,

not least because it includes the economically strongest state of the former Soviet Empire, the ex-GDR. Problems encountered by post-communist successor states, now making the transition to the free market and parliamentary democracy, are also being played out within Germany, albeit modified by participation in the prosperity of the old Federal Republic.

6 Germany's intermediary position also accounts for one peculiarity of her collective identity – the tension between, on the one hand, her inferiority complex compared with the civilizations of the South (Italy) and West (France first, and since industrialization and the growth of the parliamentary system, also England), and, on the other, her feelings of superiority, if not arrogance, towards the Slav East.

7 Belonging to both the west and south of Europe as well as the north and east, sharing the complex tensions of both, Germany never found a place in Europe which was unambiguously its own. Torn between the industrializing, liberalizing West and the agrarian, autocratic (from 1917 to 1989/91, communist) East, her central position accounted for one fundamental constant of her history – tensions, fluctuations and abrupt disjunctions. Discontinuities represent the great continuum of German history: if Faust had 'two souls in his breast', Germany always had more than two.

8 All these factors explain one unique aspect of the German Question: only the Germans, when they come together politically in a (national) state, automatically become overnight the strongest power in their region. Sooner or later they find themselves, actually or potentially, in a dominant position in Europe – and from there, as history shows time and again, the temptation is to go for further expansion of power: the foundation of the medieval German kingdom in 911, the victory over the Hungarians at Augsburg in 955 and the crowning in Rome of Otto I as Emperor in 962, are all logically closely interconnected. After the decline of the medieval Reich following the dynastic feud between the Guelphs and Staufens beginning in 1198, and the final demise of the Reich in 1806, the 'Lesser Germany' of 1871 ushered in a new hegemonic phase, which after 43 years issued in the First World War, in an attempt to convert latent into open hegemony. Inevitable defeat in 1918 by virtually the rest of the world was not something which the Weimar Republic, in the interim between Second and Third Reich, could turn to constructive political effect. Accordingly, the expansion of the Third Reich into a Greater German Reich in 1938 plunged Europe inexorably into the Second World War only one year later.

9 Oscillating between the status of power vacuum and power centre, no other people in the world has experienced so many and such extreme shifts of fortune over the last two centuries. Every occassion when the Germans were politically united has had disastrous consequences in modern times, both for themselves and for Europe: almost 700 years of being a power vacuum after 1198 ended in the three wars of German unification between 1864 and 1871, and in Bismarck's refounding of the Reich in 1871, which exploded into two World Wars; forty-five years of a divided Germany after the Second World War ended in the reunification of 1989/90, as a by-product of the Soviet collapse – a peaceful process so far, but on the threshold of a global crisis whose outcome is still open.

10 Seen from a world-historical perspective, the recent history of the Germans is unique in one further respect: only modern Germany has felt strong enough to challenge almost the whole world, twice within a mere twenty-five years, in the two world wars. The Holocaust – 'Auschwitz' – the mass murder of Jews organized by the Reich in the Second World War, represents a further enormity.

11 One discordant aspect of recent German history has been the extreme discrepancies between its power-political low points (1806, 1918/19) and high points (1871, 1914–18, 1938, 1939–42), on the one hand, and its cultural and moral high points (around 1800) and low points (1942–5; Auschwitz) on the other. There is probably no other people whose cultural high-water mark and lowest power-political ebb coincided as they did in Germany around 1800, just as their power-political zenith was accompanied by their moral nadir between 1942 and 1945.

12 Such extreme fluctuations of German power provoked all kinds of extreme emotional reaction, both individual and collective. 'German hysteria'[8] manifested itself on the Right in the hyperchauvinism of the *Reichspatrioten* at high points of German power, on the Left in anational or even antinational self-negation after each defeat. This opened the door to irrational and hysterical reactions to a German history of which people could not make sense.

13 Consequently, the course of German history was never as harmonious or as smooth as the history of stable nations tended to be. Instead, the German Question constantly fluctuated between unity and division: unity heralded future dissolution, and division the next phase of German unity (plus power). If the collective identity of long-established nation-states can be likened to a circle (as a symbol of harmony) with the capital in its centre, German collective identity may be symbolized by an ellipse, with two foci – Goethe's

Weimar and Auschwitz. Germans have to accept and cope with both.

HISTORICAL BACKGROUND TO THE GERMAN QUESTION 911–1806

Everything before the end of the Holy Roman Empire in 1806 is the prehistory of the German Question in its modern form. The founding of the German kingdom in 911 and its rapid rise as would-be renewer of the (Western) Roman Empire, followed by its long decline into a power vacuum, render visible long-term structures and processes which have governed the German Question. That is why knowledge of the prehistory, lasting some 900 years, is essential if we are to understand Germany's tribulations after 1806.

German kingdom and 'Roman' Empire: Germany as the first power centre of medieval Europe, 911/62–1198

From the early beginnings of German statehood, most of the main factors determining German history were already in evidence: with the coming together of the four East Franconian tribes (Franks, Swabians, Bavarians, Saxons) in 911 as the German kingdom, and the addition in 925 of the Lothringians/Lorrainers (about half of whom spoke German or French respectively) on both sides of the Rhine, Germany still lay on the eastern frontier of Latin Europe in terms of its cultural geography and power politics.

Everything before the founding of the German kingdom in 911, however important this prehistory may be in itself, precedes German history proper. Consequently, the development of the west Germanic tribes in the free part of *Germania* outside the Roman Empire, as well as the territories within the *limes* which later belonged to Germany; the Empire of the Merovingians and the Carolingians; the disintegration of the Carolingian Empire and the independence of the East Frankish kingdom as a product of this division in the East – the entire history of the proto-Germans before 911 – remains outside the scope of this essay. But as soon as Scandinavia was peacefully Christianized from the missionary archbishopric of Bremen, the South-East from Salzburg and the East (especially Poland in 966 and Hungary in 1000) from Magdeburg, Germany shifted into its position at the centre of Europe.

In 911/925, the boundaries of medieval Germany were roughly those of the Federal Republic before 1990, that is to say, it extended eastward as far as the Bohemian Forest and the rivers Saale and Elbe. Its main axis was the Rhine, and by extension the upper Danube. Around 1000, after the chaos of the invasions of the barbarians had been overcome, cities which had once been Roman and which were now the residences of bishops were showing signs of a renewal of municipal life, initially as centres for intercontinental long-distance trade.

The new German kingdom quickly became – relatively – the strongest power lying between the two great cultural centres of the early Middle Ages – Byzantium in the South-East and the Arab-Moorish Emirate (after 929, Caliphate) of Cordoba in the South-West. Not that the early Germans were particularly powerful in absolute terms. But in the age of feudal fragmentation, all other power groupings were even weaker for being fragmented. Lying as it did on the periphery, it was Germany's task – after the conversion of the North and East – to conquer the troublesome Hungarians at the Battle of Lech near Augsburg in 955. German victory put an end to the invasions of medieval Europe and began the process of turning the Hungarians into a sedentary and Christian people, who after 1000 became integrated in the Latin family of nations. At the same time, German victory initiated the long-term consolidation of Latin Europe: demographic and economic growth continued, in spite of interruptions and fluctuations caused by major wars, the plague and economic crises, in a thousand-year boom.

In 962, Germany's relatively pre-eminent place on the continent was recognized and symbolized by the crowning of the emperor in Rome, the foundation of the medieval German empire. Through all the internal and external changes it underwent after 962, the 'Roman Empire' (*imperium*) of the Germans remained their main source of overarching collective identity, over and above all local and regional identities. The German kingdom (*regnum*) was largely eclipsed by the splendour of the imperial crown. After the Germans had lost their common, quasi-national state with the demise of the Old Reich in 1806, but later wanted to renew it, they called it once again as a matter of course their 'Reich', or empire.

Under three dynasties (Saxon/Ottonian, 919–1024; Salian or Salic, 1024–1125; Staufen, 1152–1250) of German kings as Roman emperors, Germany was the first power centre in Latin Europe since the fall of the Western Roman Empire in 476. Missionary German archbishoprics, the adoption of intensive land development and civic constitutions as 'German agriculture' and 'German municipal law', expansion of mining, colonization of the East, the German Hansa, Teutonic Knights, universities – all these, culminating in the Reformation, extended German influence to the North and East, though without any claims being made for 'national' power such as modern German chauvinism has raised since the nineteenth century.

By conquering the Lombard kingdom of Italy in 951 and 962 and inheriting the kingdom of Lower Burgundy (Arelat) in 1033, the new *Imperium Romanum* acquired the classic structure of a great dynastic empire: Beyond its own heartland (the German kingdom) lay autonomous or vassal or largely independent client states, linked to it by the institution of feudal suzerainty which the Reich also claimed over Bohemia, and at times also over Denmark, Poland and Hungary. Such feudal bonds were not a particular problem in the Middle Ages, for they were very common. Only in the age of nationalism, when German *Reichspatrioten* naively began to equate their former Reich with the German national state in the making, did they provoke conflict with neighbouring nationalisms, if Germans made claims to regions which were predominantly non-German by appealing to medieval instances of fleeting feudal suzerainty, which were in any case only symbolic, or even fictitious.

Early erosion of central power

Behind the facade of imperial power, the decline of the Reich into a power vacuum was already under way. Its feudal character, with the decentralization typical of feudalism, gave it an extremely diffuse structure; it lacked even a recognized capital city: the Germans are the only sedentary, civilized people who for most of their history have had no capital city; only between 1871 and 1945 was Berlin capital of the Reich. Goethe thought it 'un-German' (*undeutsch*) to pursue the idea of a capital city for Germany[9].

Even more seriously: since Rome was the place where imperial power was bestowed and legitimized, German kings always had to make their way there – a journey which generally involved war with parts of Upper Italy centred around Milan and parts of Tuscany (Florence). According to feudal law, vassals of the German crown were only committed to military service within the German kingdom. In order to gain their military aid *outside* the German kingdom, the crown had to offer the princes of the Reich concessions in return. From the time of Emperor Frederick I (Barbarossa), the crown as the symbol of central power, consequently paid the price by devolving ever more royal power (*Regalien*) upon the princes.

The best example of how this mechanism worked is the Battle of Legnano in 1176. The Guelph Henry the Lion, who was Duke both of Bavaria and of Saxony, had in the course of the colonization of the East built up a position of virtually regal power as liege lord to Slav dukes in Pomerania and Mecklenburg, and as the founder of cities such as Lübeck and Munich, thereby rivalling his imperial cousin Frederick I (Barbarossa). Before the decisive Battle of Legnano, he withheld the assistance of his knights because the Emperor was unwilling to cede Goslar to him, and with it the Rammelsberg silver mine. From the edge of the battlefield at Legnano, Henry the Lion and his knights calmly watched the defeat of his royal liege, cousin and rival at the hands of the Lombard City League under Milanese leadership.

Defeat at Legnano and the Peace of Constance in 1183 meant the end of German suzerainty over Italy, which could then, its autonomy recognized, embark on its Renaissance. Henry the Lion had acted legitimately in a feudal context, for armed assistance was voluntary for vassals of the crown outside the boundaries of the German kingdom. But in 1180, Barbarossa took his revenge on Henry the Lion by destroying his position of power in the Reich as a potential rival claimant to the throne. By doing so, however, he also destroyed the beginnings of a stable territorial basis for the crown, analogous to the building of a central fiscal state in neighbouring France, which began at much the same time. Rivalry between the Staufen and Guelph dynasties sparked off civil war in 1198, precipitating Germany's decline and the second great power vacuum in Europe since 476. Latin Europe's centre of gravity shifted towards France after its victory at Bouvines in 1214.

Large-scale German colonization of the East after 1143 as a partly peaceful, partly bellicose expansion, remained somewhat diffuse. It was no longer an undertaking of the central royal or imperial power, but of regional powers (princes, cities, chivalric orders). By forcing into submission and Germanizing the politically fragmented Slavs between the Elbe and the Oder, Germany achieved a common border with Poland. On eastern 'colonial territory', *Rittergüter* ('knightly estates' or manors) remained up to 1945 as visible memorials to past conquest and colonization. Noble families remained in remarkably continuous possession of their *Rittergüter* as the ruling class (later, *Junker*) over East German and Slav peasants, whose status became progressively identical.

The medieval Reich as a power vacuum, 1198–c.1500

In time, German central power became increasingly eroded as substantial royal powers were given away to the territorial princes for the semblance of imperial grandeur. Emperor Frederick II, nominally a Staufen but in fact a south Italian, built himself a tightly controlled centralized state in his kingdom of Naples and Sicily, but left Germany north of the Alps to its own devices. He even prevented his son Henry (VII), who ruled Germany as his lieutenant, from attempting to put the power of central authority on a new footing by entering into alliance with the cities against the vassals of the crown. Frederick sealed Henry's downfall by the imperial laws of 1220 and 1231, legitimizing (if not actually facilitating) the process whereby vassals of the crown rose to become autonomous princes in their territories. The consequence was extreme political fragmentation, outwardly camouflaged by the imperial crown, whose splendour long continued to conceal Germany's power-political weaknesses.

With the downfall of Henry VII, the Germans lost their last chance to exchange the dazzling chimera of a Roman-German empire for a more pedestrian, but more substantial existence as a proto-national kingdom comparable to that of France or England in the west, or Denmark or Sweden in the north. As their state became increasingly fragmented, they were left insisting on the union of empire (with its originally at least latent claim to hegemony over Latin Europe) and kingdom – a quasi-national or proto-national kingdom of a kind which had almost disappeared. After 1806, this equation of empire (*imperium*) and kingdom (*regnum*) became one of the central problems of the German Question.

With the death of Frederick II there began the interregnum (1250/54 – 1273), 'the time without an emperor, a terrible time' (Schiller). The distant emperor disappeared into the Kyffhäuser mountain, from whence he later merged in the popular imagination with 'Frederick, the last emperor', messianic-apocalyptic bringer of future redemption, and ultimately with his more popular grandfather, the Emperor 'Barbarossa'. Until such time as the Reich rose up again whole, he would wait there with his knights. Meanwhile, regional, even local, powers were in the ascendant in the German power vacuum. As autonomous rulers, chief among them seven electors – including the King of Bohemia, most powerful imperial prince of his day – they determined Germany's structure for centuries.

In 1486, the Holy Roman Empire added the words 'of the German Nation' to its official title, but after 1495 also forsook a single modest reform which could have turned Germany into a 'normal' kingdom. The result of this attempted reform of the Reich was instead a bare minimum of common imperial authorities (the parliament, or *Reichstag*, the imperial court of justice (*Reichskammergericht*), and administrative districts for raising an imperial army). A tax for financing the reforms provoked the refusal of the Swiss Confederates. With the Swabian War and the Peace of Basle in 1499, there began the usual process of secession by peripheral regions seeking independence, in that case of Switzerland.

The agony of the Reich: from Reformation to German dualism, 1517–1789

Even before the Reformation, Germany was being pulled apart by a process which, however insignificant it at first appeared, had a cumulative effect over the centuries. In 1492/98, there began east of the Elbe a new form of intensified agrarian production, on the basis of the so-called 'second serfdom' – the antithesis of Luther's spiritual 'freedom of all Christian men': The land-owning gentry in roughly the area which had been Slav until 800/1134 developed their estates into capitalist agrarian enterprises, supplying the increasingly urbanizing, later also industrializing North West of Europe with corn. Spreading eastward, demesne farming (*Gutswirtschaft*) and second serfdom, in Russia the actual enslavement of the peasants, became the social basis for autocracy.[10] In addition to the North–South division of Germany by Reformation and Counter-Reformation, the Elbe became once again what it had been up to 800/1137 – Europe's East–West structural divide.

Reformation and Counter-Reformation merely increased the fragmentation of Germany as a state. A two fold religious boundary was superimposed on the older territorial fragmentation of the Reich. The North became predominantly Protestant (Lutheran, Calvinist), the South remained predominantly Catholic, the middle was mixed Protestant and Catholic.

All three religious wars which have taken place on German soil (including Switzerland) were sparked off in these mixed areas – the two Kappel Wars in Switzerland of 1529/31; the Schmalkalden War of 1546/47, brought to an end by the compromise of the Peace of Augsburg in 1555; and the Thirty Years War of 1618–48, brought to an end by the Peace of Westphalia in 1648. At Augsburg in 1555, the principles of tolerance and parity (the dividing up of imperial offices) sealed and regulated the split between Catholics and Protestants, while a territory's religion was determined by princely or municipal authority in accordance with the principle of *cuius regio, eius religio* – modified by the *ius emigrandi*, permitting dissenters to emigrate and to take their movable belongings with them. Parity was not extended to the Calvinists (members of the Reformed Church) until the Peace of Westphalia, nor was tolerance extended at all to those sects which had broken away at the time of the Reformation.

As in France and England, Germany's 'wars of religion' were also constitutional wars internally, and wars for power and hegemony externally. The Peace of Westphalia in 1648 – the result of Europe's first great peace congress – gave confirmation in international law to Germany's effective status as a power vacuum, ratifying its political fragmentation and formally acknowledging the rise of German princes from autonomy to near-sovereignty (*Teutsche Libertät*). Germany was now a confederation of princes and free cities, with an emperor as formal figurehead but without central government. Only in the territorial states, not in the Reich as such, could reform and modernization take place. At the same time, the Peace of Westphalia recognized by international law the sovereignty of the Swiss Confederation (virtually independent since 1499) and that of the Dutch States-General (proclaimed in 1581). Much later, around 1900, the secession of these two new national states was twisted by the Pan-Germans into their theory of *membra disiecta*, or 'amputated limbs', which had to be rejoined to the German Reich.

The Peace of Westphalia ratified the fragmentation of the Reich through a guarantee issued by the signatory powers. Subsequently, in accordance with international law, alterations to the German constitution would require the approval of all the signatory powers. This set the seal on German constitutional immobility and the Reich's inability to enact reform of its own accord. With the Peace of Teschen in 1779, Russia, too, became one of the powers guaranteeing the constitution of the Reich. At the Congress of Vienna in 1815, the international guarantee for the new German Confederation was endorsed and further strengthened, though now only by the Great Powers. This is why the Frankfurt Constitution of 1849 required the approval of Great Powers outside Germany, and why Bismarck took great care to secure their agreement at each step when founding the Reich in 1871. This constellation continued in the changed political circumstances after 1945, when the four occupying powers exercised sovereignty over Germany, and in the final phase of German unification in 1990, when the Two-plus-Four Treaty required their formal consent.

Germany's political fragmentation is well illustrated by the fact that in 1789 there were precisely 1,789 political units in the German Reich with a claim to sovereignty, ranging from the very large (Austria, Prussia), large (Saxony, Bavaria, Hanover, the Archbishopric of Cologne), and medium-large (Württemberg, most bishoprics), to the small (mini-principalities, counties, the larger imperial cities) and the smallest (abbeys, small imperial cities, imperial knights, even imperial villages). Among the positive consequences of this chaotic fragmentation were the development of federalism and the rich variety of the German cultural landscape, observed by Goethe.

It is possible in retrospect to recognize factors, even as the Old Reich came to its painful end, which later helped determine the German Question. The Thirty Years War left the Germans with a traumatic political legacy: Never again a Thirty Years War! Never again the battlefield of Europe! The consequences were clear: if Germany were not to remain a power vacuum, it would have to unite politically, becoming a power centre itself once again – 'anvil or hammer', as Chancellor von Bülow spectacularly put it at the high point of German *Weltpolitik*.

In addition, on the eastern periphery of Germany, historically on colonial lands of medieval conquest, three new power centres were emerging: Austria, Saxony and Brandenburg-Prussia. But only the powers in the South (Austria) and the North (Prussia) achieved European Great Power status. From the time of the First Silesian War (1740–2), their power struggle for hegemony in Germany determined events until 1866. German dualism became a key to the German Question: who would unite Germany – Austria or Prussia?

Even after the emergence of Austria (1683) and Prussia (1763/72) as European Great Powers, Germany remained a power vacuum, for the tension between the two German Great Powers largely paralysed their external influence. There was a double polarity: on the one hand between Austria and Prussia, on the other between them and the smaller territories of the Reich. From the first phase of French hegemonial politics under Louis XIV onwards, the non-German Great Powers had a vital interest in maintaining the German power vacuum at the centre of Europe, the better to balance their conflicting interests there. Germany as a power vacuum was a central prerequisite for the balance of power in Europe, at least since the rise and consolidation of the pentarchy – the domination of Europe by the five Great Powers.

The second major factor which accounts for Germany's transformation from a power vacuum to a power centre in 1871 is its cultural history. After humanism and the Reformation, and even more so with the economic recovery following the Thirty Years War, many political centres – courts, capitals, the larger imperial cities – developed into independent cultural centres. In competition with one another, they opened up ever-wider spheres of activity to a growing pool of talent.

This cultural pluralism – antimatter, as it were, to the missing political centralization – was to climax in the cultural explosion of German Classicism around 1800.

The end of the Old Reich under the impact of the French Revolution, 1789–1806

On the completion of the European pentarchy, with Prussia's emergence as the fifth, smallest and weakest of the European Great Powers in 1763/72, the death throes of the Old Reich which had begun in 1648 entered a new phase. Prussia had maintained itself against Austria in 1763, but only thanks to Russia's withdrawal from the Seven Years War in 1762. After 1764, Prussia was allied with Russia – one of the constants of European power politics until after 1871. Faced with the French Revolution, Austria and Prussia temporarily suspended their rivalry, but revolutionary France swept over the *ancien régime* in Germany, too, and brought down the façade of the Old Reich: in 1795, Prussia withdrew from the first Coalition War in the Separate Peace of Basle, buying for itself and northern Germany a decade of peace, during which flourished German Classicism and early Romanticism. As a substitute for a national state, the German intelligentsia cultivated a lofty philosophical cosmopolitanism, embodied by the mature Goethe, as Principal Minister of the Grand Duchy of Eisenach-Weimar, while he also stood for enlightened reforms in the individual states.

Prussia ushered in the demise of the Old Reich by agreeing in Basle to the secession of the whole left bank of the Rhine to France. In the Peace of Campoformio with Austria in 1797 and the Peace of Rastatt with the Reich in 1798, France decreed that German imperial princes who had lost territory west of the Rhine should be compensated with territory east of the Rhine. In the *Reichsdeputationshauptschluss* (Enactment of the delegates of the Empire) of 1803, the Reichstag transformed this principle into extensive mediatization and secularization: most of the smaller estates of the Reich, including all but six of the free imperial cities, lost their 'immediate' status of being directly placed under the Emperor and were absorbed by larger states ('mediatization'); so too were ecclesiastical principalities ('secularization').

In this first act of Napoleonic reorganization, middle-sized states increased in size (Bavaria, Württemberg, Saxony), rising to kingdoms, others to grand duchies (Baden, Hesse-Darmstadt). The second act followed in 1806: under Napoleon's threats, the last Holy Roman

Emperor renounced the imperial crown, to remain only Emperor of Austria. For Napoleon, the German Empire which stretched back to Charlemagne was thereby at an end, and it was now the turn of the French as the modern Franks to provide an Emperor.

2 From power vacuum to power centre
From the First to the Second Reich, 1806–1871

The death of the Holy Roman Empire gave birth to the German Question.

NAPOLEONIC INTERLUDE, 1806–1813

No sooner had the Old Reich disappeared than Prussia was ignominiously defeated by the French under Napoleon I at the twin battles of Jena and Auerstedt. These two events, and their repercussions, shaped the German Question from the outset: loss of common statehood and the collapse of Prussia – though it was Prussia which forged the new Reich in 1871, as a German national state.

Confederation of the Rhine and Prussian reforms

The end of the Old Reich was immediately preceded by the foundation of the Confederation of the Rhine in Paris and the withdrawal from the Reich of the sixteen states involved. It supplied the framework for a provisional and partial solution. As its French name, *Confédération du Rhin*, suggests, it was a confederation under the protection of Napoleon. After the Prussian débâcle, most other German states followed suit – the exceptions were Prussia, Austria, Holstein (Danish) and Pomerania (Swedish) – and demonstrated considerable potential for reform, symbolized by adoption of the legal Code Napoléon.[1] In many ways, the Confederation of the Rhine was the streamlined successor to the erstwhile Reich – but without a German emperor, and as a power vacuum. As client states of France's First Empire the states of the Confederation were eclipsed by the more dazzling and enduring resurrection and ascendancy of Prussia after 1813.

However, Prussia, the largest north German state, was a more important model for future modernizing: in reaction to the traumatic defeat of 1806, a territorially diminished Prussia launched radical structural reforms.[2] Most reformers came from outside Prussia – Stein, Hardenberg, Scharnhorst, Gneisenau. They consciously adopted elements of the French Revolution, the better to immunize Prussia against revolution through modernization. (All but) abolition of the serfdom of the peasants, freedom of the individual and of property, Jewish emancipation, freedom to exercise one's trade or choose one's profession, equality before the law, mobility (i.e. free purchasability) of land, etc., removed, or at least took the first steps towards removing, what remained of the medieval feudal order and created conditions for industrialization. Educational reform, in particular, with its three-tier system of primary school, *Gymnasium* and university, was later imitated by other German states and by Germany's neighbours to the north and the east. Army reform was no less important: the election of officers by the men of the militia and territorial reserve introduced a liberal element into the formerly hidebound Prussian army.

The Prussian reforms had the desired effect of mobilizing sufficient energies for Prussia to participate successfully in the Wars of Liberation, 1813–15. In the post-war years they spilled over into an enormous social dynamic as well: all adults were now allowed to marry freely, and the (initially only partial) emancipation of the Jews had a similar effect: for the first time they were able (up to 1933, that is) to unfold their creativity and intellectual mobility, which for centuries had been locked in the ghetto. In general, modernizing Prussia played a major part in Germany's overall rise in the nineteenth century, giving new qualitative momentum to the German Question while at the same time making the whole issue more volatile.

The German cultural explosion and beginnings of industrialization

When the German Question formally became an historical issue in 1806, German culture was at its zenith, especially German literature, philosophy and music. Her achievements became central to a developing European, then universal, culture. The Prussian reforms created the conditions for a cultural explosion: by 1800, the Germans were already the best-educated people, except, perhaps, for the Jews. With around 25 per cent of the population able to read and write, there was already a broad middle-class and aristocratic reading public for the (estimated) 3,000 newspapers and journals. The new three-tier educational system, based on universal compulsory schooling, made it possible for society to sift and give scope to talents to a greater extent than anywhere else at the time. By 1870, when England, home of the Industrial Revolution, was only just introducing universal compulsory education with its Education Act, effectively all Germans could read and write. Berlin's reformed university, founded in 1810, with its emphasis on both teaching *and* research, became a model for other universites at home and abroad.

With industrialization, two further branches of education on a more practical level were added to the academic, university-based education system: technical universities, of which Karlsruhe was the first in 1825, brought scientific principles and methods to bear on the training of engineers for the new disciplines of technology. The so-called dual system of vocational training for qualified craftsmen developed more or less parallel to this: in addition to a three-year practical apprenticeship, attendance at vocational schools one day per week, where the apprentices learned the theoretical basis of their trade, was obligatory.

After the cultural explosion came a scientific explosion, fostered primarily by the reformed universities and new technical universities. Germans were to lead the world in many subjects – often disciplines which they themselves had founded. Up to 1945, a knowledge of German was a prerequisite for study at prestigious universities in England and America in at least a dozen subjects (such as mathematics, physics, chemistry, philosophy, classical philology, archaeology, musicology), since the basic textbooks were often written in German. The many German Nobel prizewinners before 1933, often Jewish, bear witness to the pre-eminence of German scholars in the nineteenth and twentieth centuries.

The first signs of industrialization coincided with Germany's low point as a power vacuum, symbolized by the year 1806. The Continental System, which Napoleon declared from a conquered Berlin in 1806, was a trade embargo against English goods, and served effectively as a protective customs barrier, especially for the west of Germany, as the founding in Essen in 1811 of the firm of Krupp demonstrates. The technological explosion after the Napoleonic Wars saw Germany rise to become the second most important inventor nation after the USA. Rapid demographic and economic growth after 1850 had profound political and military consequences, for Germany was accumulating what was by the standards of the times an enormous reservoir of educated talent. In 1800, Germany had already been potentially the strongest country in Europe, in educational (qualitative) terms. With its explosive expansion in various fields following its cultural explosion and the Prussian reforms, it also became actually, after achieving political union in 1871, the strongest power – first on the continent, then in all Europe.

On the other hand, the Industrial Revolution[3] gave a new edge to Germany's internal socio-economic rifts. It first developed mainly in traditional economic centres at Germany's peripheries – the Rhineland in the west, Saxony in the east, with additional new industrial regions of the Ruhr and the Saar in the west, and Upper Silesia in the extreme south-east. With industrialization, the Rhine emerged from its decline in the early modern period as Germany's new economic axis, deepening the polarization with the agrarian Prussia of the Junkers east of the Elbe, while Saxony, as one of the Confederation of the Rhine states, was politically more westernized. Additional divergences between the North, going industrial more quickly and heavily, and the South, remaining predominantly agrarian, complicated matters still further: this north–south divide, symbolized by the River Main, may have been only secondary, but at times it came to have considerable psychological and political significance because of Prussia's dominance in the North.

The Wars of Liberation, 1813–1815

The Wars of Liberation saw the first political and military application of the Prussian reforms. However, the German – especially the Prussian – part in the victory over Napoleon was grotesquely overdone by the 'Borussian' school of German historians: Prussia was the smallest and weakest of the major powers in a broad alliance, with England supplying primarily the finance and Russia the army. Even in the famous Silesian Army under Marshal Blücher, two soldiers out of three were Russian. Had it not been for Napoleon's débâcle in Russia in 1812 and the support of Russia and England, the 'Prussian Insurrection' of 1813 would have been impossible. Nor could Germany alone have prevented Napoleon's comeback at Waterloo.

Nevertheless, the Wars of Liberation restored total sovereignty to the two major German powers, Austria and Prussia, and to those medium-sized and smaller German states which had been allied to France in the Confederation of the Rhine. And so the question arose in 1813 as to how Germany was to be politically reorganized. Of far-reaching importance was the promise of a constitution, which the Prussian king, Frederick Wilhelm III, had made at the start of Wars of Liberation. The fact that this promise was not honoured introduced a latent element of conflict into Prussian politics, one which escalated openly and remained virulent up to 1848.

FROM VIENNA TO BERLIN, 1815–1871

The Congress of Vienna, 1814/15

At the Congress of Vienna, after twenty-five years of French Revolution and Napoleonic Wars, the German Question became central to the reorganization of Europe. In order to re-establish the European system and the pentarchy of the five Great Powers, it became essential to regulate conditions in the major power vacuums of Europe – those with the most pressing national questions (Germany, Italy, Poland) – in order to avoid renewed large-scale war. Metternich's grand plan aimed to reconcile those nations and nationalities, stirred up by the French Revolution, with their existing dynastic monarchies, and thereby prevent them from achieving their own national state.

The three biggest national questions were linked in Vienna in a complex way: Austria annexed Lombardy and Venetia as well as Dalmatia, thereby interlocking the emerging South Slav Question with the German Question; it also annexed Galicia. Furthermore, the Polish Question remained linked with the German Question through Posen/ Poznan's incorporation in Prussia, though this was obscured by the famous compromise over Saxony and Poland, which had almost caused war between the victorious powers in early 1815: Poland was indeed partitioned once again, but the three parts were granted extensive autonomy. Prussia wanted to annex Saxony as punishment for its loyalty to Napoleon up to the Battle of Leipzig, but the other Great Powers, especially Austria, protested: Saxony was preserved, but lost approximately half its territory to Prussia. As compensation for having forgone annexation of Saxony *in toto*, Prussia received the Rhinelands, now without a ruler, where, in the words of the song *Die Wacht am Rhein* (1840), it would 'keep watch on the Rhine' for Europe against troublesome France. Thus, the most important seedbed of Germany's coming industrialization, though this was unknown at the time, fell into Prussian hands.

The Act of the Congress of Vienna had the character of a basic law for Germany, whose constitution was once again, as in the Peace of Westphalia of 1648, sanctioned and guaranteed by the signatory powers. Whilst the loose German Confederation apparently restored the static principle of sovereign states, the stipulation that constitutions based on the territorial estates (*landständisch*) were to be introduced ushered in a dynamic element which was to make for a stormy future. The wording was vague and contradictory: a constitution as such was already revolutionary, but estates (*ständisch*) suggested the pre-revolutionary *ancien régime*. Only the south German states (Bavaria, Württemberg, Baden, Hesse-Darmstadt) along with Hanover (linked to England in personal dynastic union until 1837) set up state parliaments (*Landtage*) as required, which became nurseries for the coming age of parliamentarianism. Discrepancies between popular expectations and the refusal to introduce parliamentary constitutions bred internal conflicts, especially in Prussia after 1847, which led to the revolution of 1848.

The German Confederation: between apparent power vacuum and latent power centre, 1815–1866

What German *Reichspatrioten*, such as the Reichsfreiherr vom und zum Stein, and Ernst Moritz Arndt, demanded from the Congress of Vienna as an answer to the German Question was no more nor less than the restoration of the German Reich. But the Great Powers refused in horror. For England and Russia, on the periphery of the continent, such a concentration of power at the centre of Europe was intolerable, essentially anti-European and to be feared, while the German Great Powers, Austria and Prussia, jealously guarded their own recently restored sovereignty. As a compromise between a new German Reich and total fragmentation there emerged the German Confederation, replacing the Old Reich within the same borders.

The *Deutscher Bund* was a loose confederation, without a common government or even a head of state. Its internal structure was based on Napoleon's territorial changes, with some modifications: there remained thirty-nine sovereign German states, including four free cities (Lübeck, Hamburg, Bremen and Frankfurt). The only central body was the Bundestag, a permanent congress of delegates in the old imperial city of Frankfurt. Austria's presidency of this body was unchallenged, but Prussia, from its original position as junior partner, developed the dynamic of the younger, more compact, and, in time, qualitatively stronger rival.

Basic aspects of the German Question were thrown into ever-sharper relief over the following decades, most explosively during the 1848/49 revolution. The German Confederation contained large predominantly non-German populations, especially Czechs in Bohemia and Moravia, Italians in South Tirol and Friuli and Slovenes in the far south-east of Austria. In addition, Austria and Prussia were in possession of non-German regions outside the German Confederation (Hungary, Upper Italy, Galicia, Posen), and of others with a predominantly German population (West and East Prussia). On the other hand, Hanover belonged to Great Britain (until 1837) and Holstein to Denmark (until

1864) in personal dynastic union. Consequently, the boundaries of language, people and state seldom coincided.

In terms of power politics, the German Confederation was a compromise beset with tensions and conflicts between its existing status as a power vacuum and a potential power centre. Though it contained two German and European Great Powers, Austria and Prussia, they continued to paralyse each other in the now escalating rivalry of 'German Dualism'. As Metternich's adviser Friedrich von Gentz fittingly remarked, the confederation of the *Deutscher Bund* was strong enough for defensive, but too weak for offensive purposes. The fact that Germany was relatively a power vacuum served the ends of the other Great Powers in maintaining a balance of power that was in their own interest.

Yet even the modest German Confederation was economically and militarily a latent great power, indeed a world power, as described and desired by spokesmen of the liberal National Movement even before 1848[4]. All that was lacking was political unification and the construction of a powerful navy to challenge Great Britain. Until then, German potential remained (in a positive sense) neutralized, but polarized between the industrializing, liberalizing West and the agrarian, autocratic East. German intellectual and political culture was broadly western-oriented, but numerous factors weakened the western influence under the shadow of Czarist Russia. Factors which drew Germany toward the autocratic East were the remainders of peasant dependence on Junker estate-owners east of the Elbe, the restoration of absolutism in Prussia and Austria in 1814/15, and the strong influence of Russia over Prussia and other German states arising from dynastic links, so that Marx could write polemically of Prussia as 'Russia's jackal'.

Unity and power, 1815–1848

Nevertheless, new forces were pushing beyond the limited solution imposed by the Congress of Vienna settlement, which were to destroy it in several stages. The essential elements in this west European process were nationalism as the long-term effect of the French Revolution, industrialization, the rule of law and parliament. In Germany, Romanticism and modernized versions of *Reichspatriotismus* weakened western nationalism and liberal constitutionalism.

In the generation after the Congress of Vienna, modernization brought about by incipient industrialization prepared the way for a new Reich, at first in many small, modest steps, but finally cumulating in a breathtaking dynamic. Economic growth in town and countryside, linked (after 1834) with rapid population growth and the construction of major roads and railways, the reforms in Prussia and the former states of the Confederation of the Rhine, the explosion in education, science and technology – all of these pushed towards an internal common market in Germany. Cosmopolitanism of the Classical period shifted to romantic nationalism or *Reichspatriotismus*, which combined the traditional imperial with the modern national element.

Regional customs unions from 1818 onwards prepared the way for the creation of the German Customs Union (*Zollverein*) in 1834. Gradually, all German states – the last being Hamburg and Bremen, in 1888 – became members, with one major exception: Austria. From the outset, the German *Zollverein* was led by Prussia, which, with its acquisition of provinces on the Rhine in 1815, had become Germany's strongest and most modern economic power. It refused membership to the more agrarian Austria, and blocked two later applications (1849, 1862). The *Zollverein* created the institutional framework for the industrialization of Lesser Germany under the political hegemony of Prussia, and pre-empted, in the realm of economics, the political solution of the German Question by military means, culminating in Bismarck's Lesser German Reich of 1871.

At the same time, public opinion, predominantly liberal, aimed consistently at the creation of a Greater Germany including Austria. As throughout western Europe, public opinion only reflected the views of a small minority – those who were educated, prosperous and politically active. But ultimately its influence on the ruling classes – an even smaller minority – was decisive. Liberal public opinion generally set the agenda for the 'silent majority', which only *in extremis* made its presence felt vocally, and even then usually followed where its intellectual and political leaders led – first into the revolution of 1848/49, then the patriotic war fever against France of 1870 and the foundation of the Reich in 1871.

The first German National Assembly, in the Frankfurt Paulskirche in 1848, was overwhelmingly Greater German.[5] Even left-wing opposition agreed on its political corollary – German hegemony in Europe. On the eve of the March Revolution of 1848, the liberal consensus even discussed, and after some fluctuation of opinion approved, one further inevitable corollary: that the German Reich-to-be should also build a strong fleet – aimed against Great Britain. It should join traditional overseas expansion, acquire colonies, and itself become a world power.[6]

The imperial daydreams of the Greater German Liberals had remained idle up until the revolution of 1848, and after its failure seemed to be forgotten, for decades. But they do explain why the

German middle classes at the beginning of the 1848 revolution suddenly appeared so keen on having a navy, directed initially against medium-sized Denmark, and the smooth transition, without further discussion, to *Weltpolitik* against Britain in the Wilhelmine Reich after 1896. In reality, the basic liberal consensus of the *Vormärz* before 1848 had continued during the founding of the Reich and after 1871, as it were underground, never again to be questioned. It was only half a century later that the true significance of Germany's battle fleet dawned upon the world, when Kaiser Wilhelm II took it into his own iron-clad, but faltering fists. It equally went without saying that the passionately desired new German Reich was to be a world power as well, as it were a world power-in-waiting.

Vormärz: prelude to Revolution, 1830–48

The effect of these various factors gradually came to a head in the escalating political conflicts of the pre-1848 Biedermeier period – ostensibly so cosy and settled – as the age of the post-chaise came to an end. The French July Revolution of 1830 sparked off revolutions in Belgium and Poland, and its rumblings were also felt in the form of local unrest in Germany. Those factors which determined Germany's participation in the European Revolution of 1848/49 emerged during the *Vormärz*, roughly from 1830 to 1848: a growth of the liberal and constitutional movement, and strong pro-Polish sentiments as implicit criticism of Russia's dominant role in the Holy Alliance. The main steps on Germany's path to revolution were the Hambach Festival of 1832, the attempted seizure of a Frankfurt police station (*Konstablerwache*) in 1833, the constitutional crisis in Hanover and the protest of the Göttingen Seven in 1837. Even Prussia gave in to pressure from liberal public opinion, to the extent that Frederick Wilhelm IV had to summon the United Landtag in 1847 in order to finance the railway from Berlin east to Königsberg. As an assembly of delegates from the provincial Prussian estates, the United Landtag was not yet a real parliament, but it was nevertheless a first breach in absolute monarchy. It is where Otto von Bismarck began his political career, substituting for a delegate. Tension was further increased by the agrarian crisis of 1845–47, a general economic crisis in 1847, and a particularly hard winter in 1847/48. Beginning in Upper Italy and Paris, tensions exploded in the European Revolution of 1848/49.

The Revolution of 1848/49

In the German Revolution of 1848/49, unlike in France, it was the national, i.e. political, question which was uppermost; as in Italy, it was a question of how to achieve a single (German) nation-state. In the face of the deep agrarian and economic crisis, an expanded internal common market promised to ease material need in quite concrete terms. It added urgency to the pressure for a positive answer to the German Question and to the initial mass enthusiasm in the 'mad year' of 1848 for an all-German constitution to be drawn up by the first German National Assembly, in Frankfurt's Paulskirche.

By contrast, the 'social question' – in both its older agrarian form (the last phase of the emancipation of all peasants) and its new industrial form (the rise of the industrial proletariat, the 'fourth estate') – was of only secondary interest. The national question was the dominant issue – a new Kaiser and Reich for the Germans, but also a constitution. Next came the question which had been latent since 1815, but was now painfully exposed for all the world to see: under whose leadership should the new Reich be constructed as a German nation-state – Austria's, as in the German Confederation, or Prussia's, as in the German Customs Union since 1834: *großdeutsch* or *kleindeutsch*? What seemed to be an exclusively political controversy concealed significant economic and social factors, but these are easily lost sight of when political considerations are to the fore.

In 1848, the basic consensus of the *Vormärz* period turned into concrete action: an emphatic 'Yes' to an all-German state, according to historical tradition called the 'Reich'. The nation was united in its desire for a state which encompassed every single German state, including Austria. Opinions were only divided as to its internal structure: a clear majority rapidly gained the upper hand over a small but vociferous minority of republicans and democrats (then the followers of Revolution) who aimed at a unitary, centralized republic on the French model. The majority favoured a federal monarchy, that is, a federal state (in place of the existing confederation), headed by a Kaiser, or emperor, presiding over regional monarchies and oligarchical free cities.

This first attempt at re-establishing the Reich, even a Greater German Reich, collapsed because of internal complications and contradictions of the German Question, closely linked as it was with other national questions in Europe. The basic problem was the discrepancy between the principle of national statehood for the Germans and the multinational set-up of imperial Austria: Germans wanted to see

Austria in the new Reich, but without her numerous non-German peoples. This was not an expression of nationalistic arrogance, but a realistic insight that a German nation-state containing Czechs, Hungarians, Poles, etc. would be automatically burdened with unforseeable problems. In any case, Austria as a multinational state would clearly have dominated the single-nation German Reich.

Most German Austrians, however, refused to sacrifice their dynastic state to a German 'national' Reich by giving up their non-German territories. The German aristocracy in Austria did not want to part with those non-German peasants under their control and on whom their very existence was grounded, while her bourgeoisie did not want to relinquish secure internal markets for the new industries. German Austrians were only prepared to enter a Greater Germany with all their non-German regions. Against their 'All or nothing', it was in vain that Heinrich von Gagern came up with the idea of a narrow *kleindeutsch* federal state and a wider *großdeutsch* confederation with Austria as a compromise solution. To this the Austrian Chancellor Schwarzenberg responded with his project for 'a people of 70 million' – a loosely confederated *Mitteleuropa*, without a directly elected parliament, dominated by an undivided Austrian Empire. From then on, every subsequent vision of a *Mitteleuropa* dominated by the Germans amounted to German hegemony, whether this was what they wanted or not, if only because of the quantitative and qualitative weight of *Kleindeutschland* plus German Austria plus its numerous non-German peoples.

As early as the Frankfurt Paulskirche, then, the first *großdeutsch* solution failed because of the incompatibility of a dynastic multi-national state (Austria) and a single-nation state (the Reich). In November 1848, the Austrian government recalled the Austrian members from the National Assembly in Frankfurt. This cleared the way for the *kleindeutsch* option under Prussian leadership by default. Though victorious in a National Assembly which was now only a *kleindeutsch* rump, it was blocked by the objection of Russia, which did not want to see a liberal Reich, even one under Prussian leadership. Frederick Wilhelm IV rejected the imperial crown offered to him by a delegation from the National Assembly as 'a crown of filth', and sent in Prussian troops to suppress uprisings in the Rhineland, Baden and the (Bavarian) Palatinate aimed at implementing the constitution of the Reich adopted by the Frankfurt Paulskirche.

Conflicts around Germany: Czechs, Poles, Italy, Denmark

Meanwhile, conflicts about where to draw a future Reich's borders had clearly demonstrated the potential for trouble in the German Question. German aspirations were beginning to clash with those of their neighbours, especially Czechs, Poles and Italians, who were also aiming at national unity, as well as with Denmark. At the same time, the Frankfurt Paulskirche Assembly renewed claims to three non-German regions for the future German nation-state, each on different grounds. The justification for claiming Bohemia and Moravia was that they had been closely connected with Germany since 907. Trieste, with its mixed Italian and South Slav population, was the only outlet to the Mediterranean for southern Germany and Austria. And the Duchy of Limburg had once belonged to the Old Reich. The Pan-Germans' later theory of *membra disiecta* now made its first appearance: whatever had once belonged to the Old Reich should be restored to the new German Reich. Even more explosive were claims on Posen – two-thirds populated by Poles, but belonging to Prussia – and Schleswig-Holstein – two-thirds populated by Germans, but belonging to Denmark – Holstein was even a member of the German Confederation.

František Palacky's response to an invitation to send Czech members to the National Assembly in Frankfurt, was a refusal. It was in any case a naïve invitation, or demand, since acceptance would have meant the Czechs voluntarily subordinating themselves to a German nation which was on the point of founding a new Reich. It was the Germans themselves who provoked the first phase of Czech nationalism – but a nationalism which remained content with internal autonomy, essentially right up to 1917/18.

By contrast, force was involved in the conflicts between Germans and Poles in Posen: the Prussian king had announced the reintroduction of autonomy (suspended in 1832) for the archduchy of Posen, which was to be internally divided into two regions, one to be administered by Poles and one by Germans. Under pressure from Germans in Posen, who were themselves awakening to their own nationalism, the Prussian government pushed the planned internal border ever further eastward, eventually provoking a Polish uprising in Posen as early as April 1848. The change of mind on the part of some democrats from the East, such as Wilhelm Jordan from Königsberg during the famous Poland debate of June 1848 in the Paulskirche, signalled the end of liberal enthusiasm in Germany for the Polish cause.

Like Poland, Italy also was vexed by the German Question: Austria's

Marshal Radetzky was representing broader German interests when he suppressed the national revolution in Upper Italy in 1848/49, if only to keep Lombardy and Venetia for Austria. From then on, Germany's attitude towards the Italian Risorgimento was one of ambivalence. On the one hand, the Germans supported Austria against Italian nationalism; on the other, the German national movement after 1859 took inspiration from the victory of the Risorgimento for a possible answer to its own German Question.

The eruption of the Schleswig-Holstein question at the beginning of 1848 was the most complex problem of all. Essentially, it was a question of whether German Holstein and mixed German and Danish-speaking Schleswig should remain Danish or belong to the new Germany. Since 1460, both duchies had been linked to one another in real union – 'up ewig ungedeelt' (for ever undivided) – but Holstein had remained part of the Old Reich, while joined to Denmark in personal union. Under pressure from its 'progressive' Left, the Paulskirche Assembly declared Schleswig a member of the German Confederation, and militarily supported German rebels in the duchies with volunteers and Prussian troops. When Great Britain and Russia imposed a cessation of hostilities at Malmö on 26 August 1848, radical democrats in Frankfurt protested violently: they wanted their first German war to continue, at any price.

All these conflicts around Germany continued to fester and would recur in varying forms. Overall, the first eruption of the German Question resulted in an immediate dilemma and an inability to answer it in a positive, constructive way. Consequently, the German revolution of 1848/49 brought together a range of important problems involved in the German Question and focused them to the point of conflagration. Later conflicts modified the problems left unresolved in 1848/49. The continuing tension between the *großdeutsch* and *kleindeutsch* solutions to the German Question permeates the extreme fluctuations of subsequent German history. In a wider European, even universal, context Germany in 1848/49 demonstrated for the first time the general discrepancies between the traditional concept of multi-ethnic dynastic Empire and modern Nation, which have wrought havoc ever since – witness Bosnia and Chechnya in our own time.

Post-revolutionary war struggles, 1849/50

The facile cliché of the 'failed' bourgeois revolution of 1848/49 does not do justice to the momentous event: as so often in history, behind the back of the apparent victor the future victory of the defeated party was already in the making. Although the Prussian constitution of 1848 was imposed from above, and preserved the power of the throne with its infamous three-class voting system, even so it was a concession to the revolution and provided a constitutional framework for the future rise of the liberal bourgeoisie.

In addition, from 1850 onwards, the usual period of reaction after a revolution coincided with a new economic boom, during which Germany's industrialization really took off. New material prosperity was of political advantage primarily to the liberal bourgeoisie, which subsequently spearheaded the national movement working towards a new Reich. A concrete motive was emerging: a common German market which promised industrialization – more than just the customs union of the German *Zollverein*.

At the same time, Austria and Prussia resumed their jockeying for position in the restored German Confederation, though now with an increased awareness of their political rivalry. The question was still the one which the Paulskirche Assembly had left open-ended: should there be a single state for all Germans? Every initiative was just a variation on this same basic theme.

Into the vacuum of disappointed hopes after the failure of Frankfurt's *kleindeutsch* solution, Prussia, together with Saxony and Hanover, launched the first post-revolutionary project, vying with Schwarzenberg's *Mitteleuropa*: the *Dreikönigsbund* (three kings' alliance) of 26 May 1849. Its aim was to save at least retrospectively the original all-German consensus of March 1848 by combining it with the outcome of the Paulskirche Assembly: in addition to a (*kleindeutsch*) Reich under Prussian leadership there would be a 'German Union'. As a confederation between the new Reich and Austria in its entirety, it would link the non-German parts of the Habsburg monarchy to a Greater Germany after all. A constitution and a parliament would give the German Union a constitutional foundation. In 1850, at Prussia's initiative, the Erfurt Union parliament actually came into existence and accepted the planned constitution, but Austrian pressure ensured that the constitution was confined to Prussia, and the Frankfurt Bundestag was reconvened.

Prussia's position was further weakened by the Treaty of Olmütz in 1850. After trying in vain to intervene in Electoral Hesse's constitutional struggle, Prussia withdrew when threatened with war by Austria and Russia. Obliged to give up her plans for the Union, she returned to the Frankfurt *Bundestag*. But Bismarck became Prussian minister to the Confederation. He refused to put up with Prussia's traditional role as junior partner to Austria's presidency, and opened a campaign of needle-pricks against Austria, the presiding power of the German Confederation.

Crimean War and Prussian Army conflict, 1853–1862

After the Revolution of 1848/49, the next stage on the way leading to the foundation of the Reich was the Crimean War of 1854–56. In this coalition war of the liberal West (Britain, France, Piedmont-Sardinia) for the preservation of the Ottoman Empire against autocratic Russia's permanent expansion, both sides wooed the two German great powers to enter the war on their side. Had this happened – bringing all the European Great Powers in simultaneous conflict with each other – there would have been a First World War in 1854.[7]

But both the German Great Powers, for different reasons, kept out of the Crimean War. Though Austria felt its own interests affected by Russian expansion in the Balkans, it was still so weak from the Revolution that it shrank from the risk of war. Austrian statesmen could already see clearly what the consequences of any large-scale war would be for Austria – national and social revolution, as was indeed to come about in late November 1918 after the First World War.

In Prussia, the explosive dynamics of the tension between its eastern, conservatively agrarian part and its western, industrializing and liberalizing part, which had first shown up internally in the Revolution of 1848/49, were now having an external effect: '*Ostelbien*' – the reactionary part east of the Elbe – wanted to follow Russia; whereas the more modern, industrializing '*Westelbien*' (to give it a name it never in fact had), with the additional support of liberal conservatives under Moritz von Bethmann Hollweg (the grandfather of the later Chancellor Theobald von Bethmann Hollweg) and grouped around his journal *Wochenblatt*, tended towards the West. Since both parts were of roughly equal strength, the result was internal deadlock and external paralysis: like Austria, Prussia, too, remained neutral.

Yet the Crimean War was of great significance for the further development of the German Question. Piedmont-Sardinia under Cavour, the Italian Bismarck, went on from its alliance with France and the Italian War of 1859 to achieve victory for the Risorgimento in 1859/61. The new Italian nation-state set a precedent which in 1859 spurred on the national movement in Germany to reorganize along the lines of the *Società Italiana* in the *Nationalverein* as the liberal pressure group for national unity. Austria was further weakened, especially in Germany, by her defeat at the hands of the French and the soon-to-be-united Italians.

Perhaps even more importantly, after the Crimean War, Britain and Russia withdrew from the continent in order to concentrate on internal reforms and imperial expansion outside Europe. They left behind a relative power vacuum in Europe, with France facing the German Question in isolation, creating the essential external framework for Bismarck's foundation of the Reich, since the German national movement could now surmount both internal (constitutional) obstacles and external obstacles (international law).

When the reactionary period had come to an end, the 'new era' ushered in the first liberal phase in Prussia's history under the Prince Regent, subsequently King Wilhelm I. His aim was to set Prussia on 'moral conquests' in Germany by taking over the political leadership in Germany with popular acclaim – a 'Prussian-liberal' answer to the German Question. Defeat in the Italian War of 1859 exacerbated Austria's chronic crisis since 1848/49. While Prussia was geared to war against France on the Rhine front, trial mobilization exposed serious organizational shortcomings in the army which only comprehensive reform would rectify.

The Prince Regent (after 1861, King Wilhelm I) wanted to strengthen the standing conscript army at the expense of the territorial reserve militias, the *Landwehr* and *Landsturm*, both of which elected their own officers. By weakening the elective element in the Prussian Army, the crown provoked the opposition of the liberal majority in parliament, culminating in its refusal to ratify the military budget. The army and constitutional crisis drove Prussia to the brink of civil war, and had two decisive consequences for the German Question: Bismarck's assumption of power as Prussian prime minister in 1862, as a means of avoiding civil war, and his creation of an instrument, after army reform had been put into effect, with which Prussia could henceforth make not moral, but military conquests in Germany as well. He was prepared to use this instrument to achieve the foundation of the Reich. The moral which he publicly drew from the revolution of 1848/49 was: 'Great events are not decided by parliamentary majorities, but by blood and iron.'

Bismarck and the three Wars of Unification, 1862–1871

As prime minister, Bismarck took full advantage of what was an ideally propitious situation: internally, thanks to the liberal national movement, pressure for a German common market, and Prussia's growing importance as Germany's strongest industrial and military power; externally, because of Great Britain's lack of interest and the relative isolation of Russia and France on the continent since the Crimean War. This resulted in the three Wars of Unification: against Denmark in 1864, Austria in 1866, and France in 1870/71. Even if the 'Iron Chancellor' had not had a fixed master plan from the outset, all the causes for conflict were nevertheless linked to the German Question. As Bismarck acknowledged, the war which Prussia fought, alongside Austria, against Denmark in 1864, was linked to the Schleswig-Holstein Question that had been left unresolved in 1849. And its results provided a welcome pretext (Bismarck: 'Anknüpfungspunkt') for breaking with Austria almost immediately.

Complications arising from the condominium of Austria (Holstein) and Prussia (Schleswig), together with difficulties over a constitution for future Germany, escalated in 1866 to the 'German War'– Prussia vs. Austria and the German Confederation. After victory at Königgrätz, Prussia followed Bismarck's advice and did not press for the acquisition of land at Austria's expense, but made up for this with extensive annexations in Germany itself (Hanover, Electoral Hesse, Nassau, Frankfurt). Territorially, Prussia had filled the gap between its lands east of the Elbe and those west of the Elbe.

More crucially, with the abolition of the German Confederation, Austria was excluded from Germany and pushed more forcibly than ever before to turn its attentions towards the Balkans. As usual after a serious defeat, its crisis was exploited by Hungary in the *Ausgleich*, or 'Compromise', of 1867, which divided old Austria into the Dual Monarchy of Austria-Hungary. This settlement also put the ruling German minority in Austria on the defensive. In particular, from around 1835 onwards, the Germans in Bohemia were looking increasingly towards the patriotic national movement in what would become the Reich, while at the same time severing their older, Bohemian links with the Czechs.[8]

Bismarck, meanwhile, created the North German Federation as a transitional step towards a later *kleindeutsch* Reich. Secret offensive-defensive alliances with the southern states of Bavaria, Württemberg and Baden smoothed the way for war with France. Political continuity of a sort was preserved, for Bismarck saw to it that the constitution of the North German Federation was essentially an adaptation of the 1849 Frankfurt constitution of the Reich, with some modifications in step with the changed times.

The Franco-Prussian War of 1870/71 was ostensibly sparked off by the purely dynastic question of who should succeed to the Spanish throne. In fact, this concealed the German Question in all its problematic complexity. Emperor Napoleon III had set himself up as a champion of national movements throughout Europe (echoing, not for the first time, his uncle Napoleon I, as well as the French February Revolution of 1848 with, under Lamartine, its revolutionizing policy towards other nationalities.[9] The plan was to weaken Austria, in order to strengthen France, by revolutionizing nationalities which lacked a corresponding nation-state. New nation-states were to make up for France being isolated in Europe. Napoleon III had successfully intervened in Italy in 1859 on behalf of the Risorgimento. For geographical reasons, however, it had proved impossible for the French to repeat this success in 1863/64 by intervening on behalf of the Poles in their January Uprising against Russia.

A dynastic alliance between Germany and Spain in 1870 conjured up French memories of 'encirclement' by Habsburgs at the time of the Spanish Marriage in 1496 and from Charles V's day onwards. By clever diplomacy and by influencing public opinion (the Ems dispatch) over the issue of the Hohenzollern candidature for the Spanish throne, Bismarck so provoked his adversary Napoleon III that the French Emperor was tricked into rushing into the waiting bayonets of the *furor teutonicus*. What, more than anything else, caused the sudden surge of *Reichspatriotismus*, even – indeed especially – in southern Germany, was what Bismarck, and consequently all of Germany, trumpeted out to be the insulting behaviour of the French ambassador on the spa promenade at Bad Ems towards the Prussian king – who, in fact, had not felt at all insulted by Count Benedetti.

But in the meantime Germany had outstripped France, both quantitatively (in terms of population) and in many ways also qualitatively (level of industrialization, military training, education, infrastructure, railways). In addition, German maps were better, for German geographers and cartographers now led the world.[10] All these factors facilitated a speedier German deployment and rapid victory in the Franco-Prussian War of 1870/71 which united Germany. Fighting in isolation without allies, France suffered her débâcle. Russia neutralized Austria's desire to exact revenge for Sadowa (Königgrätz) by threatening war against Austria-Hungary, if the Dual Monarchy were to attack Prussia.

Like the German War of 1866, the Franco-Prussian War could have been over in six weeks, with the capitulation of Napoleon III at Sedan on 2 September 1870. In victory, however, the victor's appetite grew: recovery of Alsace and Lorraine became an additional war aim of the German national movement, one which was resisted by the new people's armies and *franc-tireurs* of the new Provisional Republic under Leon Gambetta. While Paris was still besieged, Bismarck negotiated the proclamation of the Emperor in the Galerie des Glaces at Versailles on 18 January 1871 – effectively the foundation of the Second German Reich. After the bitterest, bloodiest and longest phase of the Franco-Prussian War, Germany annexed Alsace-Lorraine without holding a plebiscite or granting it internal autonomy. It was the forced return of Alsace-Lorraine – what was later to be called its 'repatriation' *heim ins Reich* as one of the Old Reich's 'lost limbs' – which really anchored the enmity between Germany and France in a sea of blood.

3   Germany as a power centre
Second and Third Reichs, 1871–1945

The foundation of the Reich in 1871 seemed to have answered the German Question once and for all: in the new imperial Reich the Germans now had their nation-state, even though the Austrians had been excluded. Its borders had been drawn unambiguously. After three wars of unification, Germany had once again risen to become a power centre, though the annexation of Alsace-Lorraine was a potentially explosive, but self-inflicted handicap. With the apparent or formal disappearance of the German Question, the foundation of the Reich in 1871 and rapid transformation of Germany from a power vacuum to Europe's central power centre opened up what some historians in the old Federal Republic, critical of German nationalism, from Fritz Fischer in 1961 onwards, called a new continuity.

This continuity of German power politics under an imperial banner between 1871 and 1945 – whether Second or Third Reich – posed the question of how the Germans would use their new power. It is therefore imperative, for an understanding of the next phase of the German Question in the narrower sense of the term (1945–90), to explain first how the excessive power of the new Reich – in accordance with the dialectic of intention and inverse effect – was already preparing for Germany's next division – via the 'Struggle for Mastery in Europe' (A.J.P. Taylor), which plunged the world into two world wars.

THE SECOND GERMAN REICH, 1871–1918

Internal structure of the *Kaiserreich*

The question as to the new Germany's internal structure had also been settled – it was to be a federal monarchy. While the Reich embodied an enormous concentration of power, it was not the unitary centralized state which the democratic left had always demanded, but which would have been at variance with political tradition since the demise of the Old Reich. Under a common roof, the German princes and free cities (Lübeck, Hamburg, Bremen) not only retained their internal autonomy, they were the formal representatives of the sovereignty of the German Reich, conceived as a federal state. In reality, however, Prussia – the largest state – was by far the most influential, a fact given institutional form in the personal union of the Prussian King and the German Kaiser, with the Prussian *Ministerpräsident* generally also becoming Imperial Chancellor.

Germany was a liberal, constitutional monarchy on the western model, based on the rule of law, even if it lagged behind the parliamentary monarchies (Britain, France, the Netherlands, Belgium and the Scandinavian monarchies) and the parliamentary republic (France). Prussia east of the Elbe in particular – a stronghold of reactionary politics – retained its ascendancy over court, state and constitution, but above all over the army. Though the crown was still predominant, the new Germany was far from being an 'authoritarian nation-state'.[1] The constitutional German state rather stood somewhere between liberal parliamentarianism in the West and autocratic Russia in the East, beset with many internal divisions and getting into trouble from outside if unsatisfied with its enormous achievements.

In many respects, Germany's 'special path' was not yet clear – and can perhaps at best be reconstructed only in retrospect. Even the resort to war to settle the German Question was not exceptional for the times: *all* Europe's national questions were resolved by war – either directly as a war aim, or indirectly as the consequence of a major war.

But spiritually, the future had already begun. By 1900, the educated classes in Germany saw themselves embodied in Goethe's Faust, and were in part right to do so. Faust's urge to discover 'what holds the world together' broke all the boundaries of traditional knowledge. The revolution in the natural sciences anticipated the subsequent catastrophes of the twentieth century – from Nietzsche's 'death of god' via Planck's quantum leaps and Einstein's relativity theory to the atom bomb. The arts, especially painting and music, but also the increasingly popular literature of science fiction, reflected the tensions of the day and projected them into an uncertain future.[2]

The self-destructive dynamism of continued expansion

What was special about the use of military force to impose the *kleindeutsch* solution of 1871 was consequently not war itself, but its specific quality: three wars in quick succession, fought single-handed, against one medium-sized power (Denmark) and two European Great Powers (Austria and France). All other wars fought to settle questions of nationhood, particularly those of Italy and the South Slavs, required help from Great Powers. Italy may have been formally a Great Power herself, but she remained a lightweight and was never fully accepted by the other Great Powers as an equal. Poland profited from the First World War for her national resurrection. The Germans alone were quantitatively and qualitatively powerful enough to exploit a favourable situation – after the break-up of the Crimean coalition in 1856 – to fight for and win their national unity by going it alone.

In 1871, a newly unified Germany rose overnight as the strongest power on the European continent. Germany's meteoric industrialization perpetuated Russia's qualitative backwardness on the periphery of the continent, in the long run also in power-political terms, especially since Russia's own industrialization, imposed from above, became inextricably linked with social revolution from below. The Reich quickly emancipated itself from being what Prussia had traditionally been: a client state of Russia. As a safety measure, Bismarck wanted to keep at least 'a wire to St Petersburg' open for as long as possible, even making early concessions to Russian interests in 'the Orient' – namely, that part of the Balkans which was still Ottoman, and Constantinople.

As the age of imperialism got under way, Britain initially maintained its traditional lead both as an industrial power and as a naval and colonial power. It was safe from German expansion as long as the Reich did not build a navy which could compete with its own. But when, in 1898, Germany began to build a battle fleet of such strength that it only made sense as an instrument to be deployed against Britain, antagonism between the two nations was inevitable,[3] the more so since Germany in the years up to 1914 was catching up with and overtaking Britain in important areas of its economic development.

There was already built into the *kleindeutsch* settlement of the German Question in 1871 a momentum of its own towards the *großdeutsch* solution, that became reality in 1938 – with an Austrian in charge of the Reich. Continued growth of population – from 38 million in 1871 to 64 million in 1914 – and economic growth were an additional dynamic, pressing for further expansion as every new power centre had done. Consequently, Germany's geographical position in the centre of Europe became more volatile than ever, though at first this remained veiled since the German Question appeared to have been resolved in 1871. In fact, it rumbled on underground, producing conflicts which were to culminate in the First World War.[4]

The idea that 'Modern Germany was born encircled' – as an American historian somewhat unfortunately, though with the best intentions, recently put it[5] – can be formulated in a more functional way, avoiding the emotive term 'encircled' with its historical bias, if we look objectively at the map of 1871. On account of its central position, Germany was the only Great Power which bordered on all the other four Great Powers: France, Austria-Hungary and Russia on the continent, Great Britain across the North Sea. If Germany wanted to expand, it could only do so at the expense of one or other of the Great Powers, and risked all the others combining to prevent the Reich converting its latent hegemony into an open one. Every historical precedent demonstrates that any Great Power, however formidable, would be defeated by a coalition of all the others. If Germany were to attempt to expand overseas through *Weltpolitik*, it would clash with Britain, if only for the simple geographical reason that Britain as an island kingdom blocked Germany's path into the Atlantic, her gateway overseas.

Bismarck may have declared Germany to have become 'saturated' after 1871, but in reality the *kleindeutsch* Reich already contained the explosive seeds of further expansion beyond its relatively modest borders. If history teaches anything, it is that the other Great Powers would not simply abdicate and voluntarily submit to the more powerful and impetuous newcomer on the European and world stage. It was inevitable that further expansion and its self-defeating consequences would throw up the German Question again. That is why Bismarck had no great faith in the durability of his work, however dazzling it appeared. He was plagued by visions of the Reich's collapse as a result of its being overextended in its difficult central position – the *cauchemar des coalitions* became the nightmare of a war on two fronts.

Kleindeutsch-großdeutsch: the latent initial stages of Pan-German expansion

The threat of expansion, linked to the German Question, was already latent in the continuing tension between the *kleindeutsch* and *großdeutsch* solutions. Although the complications which led to the failure of the *großdeutsch* solution in 1848/49 had been internal German ones, it nevertheless remained a potential alternative – it was both a temptation and a threat. In German history books and other German accounts, plenty of references are made (in all innocence, and, in formal terms, accurately) to the fact that Bismarck's *kleindeutsch* Reich did not contain all the Germans, but 'only' some two-thirds of them, while the other third lived outside the Reich, mostly in Austria-Hungary. But here, precisely, was the rub: if the Austro-Hungarian Empire were to disintegrate – something which its rulers themselves feared from, at the latest, 1854 onwards as the consequence of a major war – then the German component would be free to seek integration (*Anschluß*) with the *kleindeutsch* Reich, and was likely to do so. Thus, every attempt to bring about *kleindeutsch* German leadership of central Europe unavoidably contained a latent *großdeutsch* dynamic as an explosive potential, even within the framework of the Habsburg monarchy, as long as it existed.

The Compromise of 1867 transforming the Austrian Empire into Austria-Hungary was itself a first step towards dissolution, for the Dual Monarchy was in effect a very fragile confederation of the two virtually independent parts of the Empire – Hungary (Transleithania) and Austria (Cisleithania).[6] Moreover, the Hungarians, with their strict policy of Magyarization drove their minorities, especially Romanians in Transylvania and South Slavs in Croatia, into open opposition.[7] The Germans in Cisleithania, politically still the dominant group, made up a mere third of the total population, and this put them on the defensive against the rising nationalism of Czechs and Italians in particular.

As the Austro-Hungarian Empire became weaker, the feeling among its German population that they were an impotent minority, especially in the lower strata, who had only their language and Germanness to distinguish them from other nationalities, bred *großdeutsch* sentiments in a vaguely but stridently Pan-German hue. Adolf Hitler, who came from the poor *Waldviertel* region close to the Czechs, was only one among many products of this particular constellation – it was a situation which would have far-reaching collective repercussions. The 'German National-Socialist Workers' Party' (in German: DNSAP), founded by German workers in the border regions of Bohemia (later to be known as the Sudetenland) in early 1918, provided the name (after a slight change in the suggestive order of names) for Hitler's NSDAP in Munich. The DNSAP was originally founded for German workers in opposition to the *Czech* National-Socialist Party and the international (Marxist) Socialist Workers' Party, namely Social Democracy, thus becoming the 'German National Socialist Workers' Party'.

Outside Austria-Hungary, Germans resident in present-day Estonia and Latvia also wanted to join the German Reich soon after 1871. They had been the top stratum of society, socially and economically above the Estonians and the Latvians since the days of the Teutonic Knights, as Baltic barons on the land after 1237 and in the cities as the bourgeoisie. In the nineteenth century they were exposed to increasing pressure for Russification, and after the first Russian Revolution of 1905 also to pressure from a Latvian peasants' revolution. Bismarck's desire to retain Russia's friendship was reason enough for him to turn down the German Balts' overtures to join the Reich after 1871.

On the other hand, there were forces in the *kleindeutsch* Reich which demanded the more extreme *großdeutsch* solution. Their name – Pan-Germans (*Alldeutsche*) – derives from the central plank of their programme – the unification of *all* Germans in a powerful German Reich. Their Austrian equivalent were the Greater Germans (*Großdeutsche*), who around 1900 were extremely influential under Karl von Schoenerer and Karl Lueger. The Pan-Germans represented the most chauvinistic wing of German *Reichspatriotismus*. Unlike in Austria, their social base in the German Reich was an elevated one: the cream of the educated classes, leading businessmen and civil servants were sympathetic, initially including even the greatest intellect in the Wilhelmine Reich, Max Weber, who started as a liberal Pan-German.

Pan-German policy was a covert declaration of war against all powers with German minorities, especially Austria-Hungary and Russia. It is significant that when the Pan-Germans established themselves as an organization in 1890, it was in protest against the Zanzibar-Heligoland Agreement concluded under Caprivi and signalling moderation in overseas expansion. Consequently, they first appeared as extreme advocates of forceful imperial expansion under the banner of *Weltpolitik*. In his famous inaugural lecture in Freiburg in 1895, Max Weber supplied the enthusiastically acclaimed programmatic formula justifying German *Weltpolitik*:

> We have to understand that the unification of Germany was a youthful prank, and a costly one for the nation to have committed at its age, one it should have left undone if its intention was to mark the end, rather than the beginning, of German *Weltmachtpolitik* [world politics].[8]

Only later did the Pan-Germans spell out clearly what their Pan-Germanism meant in a European context, and this they propagated quite openly: in addition to those Germans living in closely knit settlements attached to the Reich, especially in the hereditary territories of the Austrian emperors and in what was later called the Sudetenland, there were also Germans in scattered settlements stretching throughout east and south-east Europe, even as far as the Volga and the Caucasus. Their unification in a single German Reich either entailed their resettlement or repatriation, or else incorporation of substantial non-German minorities in the German Reich along with them – 'minorities', which constituted majorities in their own regions. In addition, there was the demand for the return of 'lost limbs' (*membra disiecta*) – the Netherlands and German-speaking Switzerland – which had broken away from the Old Reich at the beginning of the early modern period, though their independence was only internationally recognized in 1648.

The Pan-Germans' extreme aspirations evaded the narrower parameters of the German Question, and anticipated the notion of 'living space' (*Lebensraum*). It was Karl Haushofer's geopolitical reflections and what others, with logical consistency, subsequently deduced from them which accustomed the German people to this idea of expansion – one which Hitler made his own and attempted to implement. The Pan-Germans were increasingly aware that their goals would not be achieved without a major war, and they urged that Germany should be prepared for such a war and ready to wage it at the most propitious moment.[9] However distasteful or embarrassing they may have been to German apologia after the First or Second World Wars, the Pan-Germans were not just the lunatic fringe of the Right. They drove the logic of German national and imperial unity to its bitter end – at first only verbally, but soon also militarily.

External aspects of the German Question: variants of the *großdeutsch* solution

Against the background of the Pan-Germans' programme, seen as a reaction to the *kleindeutsch* character of Bismarck's Reich, the *großdeutsch* response to the German Question – if we include the historical experience of two (German) world wars and their consequences – can be broken down into three variants:

1 Unification with closely knit German settlements bordering on the Reich – essentially *kleindeutsch* Reich plus German-speaking Austria plus Sudetenland. This was the mini-*großdeutsch* variant of 1848 as a first starting-point, achieved by Hitler (as a transitional stage) in 1938.

2 The maxi-*großdeutsch* solution, by contrast, would be the unification of '*Kleindeutschland*' and all of Austria, including the non-German parts, as envisaged by the Austrian Germans in 1848. Schwarzenberg's plans for a *Mitteleuropa* in 1850 were a theoretical continuation of this, and during the First World War, for Germans in the Reich, it was an umbrella for sweeping annexation plans and war objectives which would have reduced Austria-Hungary to a client state of Germany. The first steps towards its realization came with Hitler's Greater German Reich, which established a Reich

Protectorate over Bohemia and Moravia and annexed the Memel
territory and parts of Poland.

3 The 'super-*großdeutsch*' solution was the 'Greater Germanic Reich
of the German Nation' proclaimed by Himmler when Germany's
power was at its height in the Second World War, for the vast territories which came under the rule of the Greater German Reich had
German minorities (*Volksdeutsche*, or 'ethnic Germans'), some of
whom were resettled 'home in the Reich' (*heim ins Reich*) and all of
whom were treated as citizens of the Reich. Since the Pan-Germans
had already envisaged this solution before the First World War,
Hitler was their heir.

For want of such an analysis of the nuances involved in each of the
three *großdeutsch* options, the word itself degenerated after 1945,
becoming a negatively loaded catchword. Honecker, for instance, used
it during the death throes of his GRD *vis-à-vis* Kohl's liberal-
conservative Federal government, which (unlike the SPD) retained its
commitment to a common German citizenship right up to the end, and
consequently its responsibility for the citizens of the GDR.

Internal aspects of the German Question: the Reich and 'enemies of the Reich'

Aware of the fragility of his predominantly Protestant Reich, Bismarck raised the German Question within Germany itself under a new
guise: that of the struggle against 'enemies of the Reich' – Poles,
Danes, Guelphs, Alsatians and Lorrainers, and those Catholics
involved in 'ultramontane' (= beyond the mountains – the Alps – i.e.
Rome-oriented), 'political' Catholicism, represented in the *Zentrum*
party, as well as the Social Democrats. German anti-Semitism in the
years after 1878, though neither initiated by Bismarck nor encouraged
by him, nevertheless arose from the same kind of national logic. To be
a 'normal German citizen', it seemed you had to be Protestant and
Prussian, otherwise you were suspected of being an 'enemy of the
Reich'.

The sum total of such 'enemies of the Reich' accounted for a sizeable
proportion of the population: apart from the Guelphs, they all had
links with factors beyond the Reich – with the Polish Question (still
merely latent in 1871), with Denmark, France, the Pope in Rome, or
international socialism. Though German Jews increasingly felt themselves to be German, a growing number of anti-Semites thought they
were part of a 'world-wide Jewish conspiracy'.

There were Poles in Posnan and West Prussia (which Prussia had acquired through the partitions of Poland) whom the German Reich had taken over from Prussia. They were (and are) predominantly Catholic, and the Polish and Catholic factors combined to present Bismarck with both internal and external political problems: Bismarck's *Kulturkampf* against the Catholic *Zentrum* initially targeted only those Catholic Poles living in the areas of Upper and Lower Silesia which had Polish populations who voted for the *Zentrum*. He thereby opened in Posnan and West Prussia a new phase in the ethnic struggle against the Poles in order to Germanize them under administrative pressure. But this merely provoked resistance from below and strengthened the very nationalism which repression was intended to quash.

The Poles in Posnan (two-thirds of the population) and West Prussia (one-third of the population) organized socially and politically. In order to hold their own against the domineering Germans, they stepped up their older forms of modernization, the 'organic work' (*Praca Organiczna*) since 1838, which had provided them with a constructive alternative to the strategy of rebellion after the November Uprising of 1830/31 had failed. This became the basis of their claim for a future national state of their own through active, and successful, participation in the early stages of industrialization. After the failure of the January Uprising in 1863/64, the concept of *Praca Organiczna* was also taken up by Russian Congress Poland. Since the Poles in the German Reich participated in the improvement of German educational standards, those in the Prussian *Ostmark* became the best educated and best organized of all three zones in partitioned Poland.

Germany's problems with the Danes in north Schleswig were less serious, but were a reminder that the German Reich had been founded as a nation-state against the new principle of self-determination. The Reich refused to carry out the plebiscite in Schleswig provided for in the Peace of Prague in 1866 until compelled to do so by defeat in 1918 and the Treaty of Versailles.

Alsace-Lorraine's European dimension was nothing short of dramatic: in the extreme fragmentation and weakness of the Old Reich during the sixteenth and seventeenth centuries, these areas had been gradually absorbed by France, and they were still largely bilingual. Since the French Revolution, even those Lorrainers and Alsatians whose language and culture were German had felt they belonged to France politically and ideologically. The annexation of Alsace-Lorraine in the Peace of Frankfurt in 1871 was a heavy blow for France. Even more telling was the fact that the Reich did not allow a plebiscite of the affected population to take place, but only offered a diluted form of the option: those who chose France could emigrate to France with their movable belongings. Over 10 per cent of the population chose to do so.

Even so, in the long run, France would probably have come to terms with the loss of Alsace-Lorraine, provided Germany had granted its new province full autonomy and equal rights, trusting to the power of time and peaceful assimilation. Instead, however, Alsace-Lorraine was given the inferior status of a special region (*Reichsland*), ruled by a Governor directly from Berlin, with soldiers, mainly of the Prussian army, stationed there. The limited autonomy granted in 1911 came too late. France's almost permanent opposition to Germany between 1871 and 1914 was a logical consequence of the annexation of Alsace-Lorraine.

Even ostensibly internal German areas of conflict had an external dimension: the *Kulturkampf* against 'political' Catholicism was directed against the Pope, whose claim to infallibility had just been accepted by the Vatican Council in 1870. What Bismarck actually achieved, however, was the prolonged alienation of the third of the German population who were Catholic. Only after the *Kulturkampf* had been wound down did the disgruntlement also gradually abate, while the *Zentrum* became the very epitome of a party of the middle, holding the balance of power in the *Reichstag*.

The German 'Jewish Question' was potentially even more explosive: were Jews in Germany – the oldest group of people on German soil for whom there is written documentation (an edict of Constantine in AD 321 enlisting Jews in Cologne in the city's administration) – also Germans in the sense of the German Question? This was not a specifically German question, for all new nationalisms after 1789 (except the Italian and Greek) were anti-Semitic. But in Germany the response, an increasingly negative and destructive one, took on a self-destructive dynamic all of its own.[10]

At the Congress of Vienna, the German bourgeoisie in the remaining free imperial cities, above all Frankfurt and Bremen, had once again partially restricted the emancipation of the Jews granted in the Napoleonic era. In 1869, shortly before the founding of the Reich, the *Reichstag* of the North German Federation again removed most of these restrictions. Consequently, Germany in the nineteenth century became a cultural, academic and economic Eldorado for German Jews: nowhere else could they develop their talents so fully, nowhere else did they so identify with the culture of their country as in Germany, which many came to look on as a 'New Jerusalem'. Most Jews thought of themselves as Germans, even if they remained true to Judaism as a religion.

German anti-Semitism began in 1878 as a reaction to the world economic crisis of 1873 and was at first remarkably low key. In the German Reich of Bismarck and Wilhelm II its consequences were conceivable only in the broadest terms – the hopes of Pan-German anti-Semites, or the fears of sensitive Jews such as Franz Kafka in Prague, a city exposed in equal measure to German and Czech anti-Semitism. Nevertheless, during this first, still seemingly harmless upsurge of German anti-Semitism, one left-wing liberal member of the *Reichstag* was already shrewdly warning in 1881 of the consequences of the 'racial question' which 'will only end with the mass slaughter of the Jews'.[11]

Self-destructive in a different way was Bismarck's battle with the Social Democrats over the Socialist Law of 1878–90. Social democracy considered itself part of an international protest movement. One powerful ingredient was its doctrine of salvation – left-wing, secularized, dualistic and millenarian – which aimed to construct a future socialist state as the New Jerusalem on earth prophesied in the Book of Revelation. Socialism as 'fundamental opposition' (Bendikat) and a prescient vision of the great 'mayhem' (Bebel) to come, the earthly apocalypse, the collapse in final catastrophe of a corrupt world, a secularized Armaggedon ('Then comrades to the struggle, and the last fight let us face. The Internationale unites the human race.') – this all gave socialism a transcendental dimension beyond practical politics.[12] Bismarck, the pragmatic Protestant, mainly responded with repression and by attempting to separate the apocalyptic-cum-revolutionary wing of social democracy from its pragmatic-cum-conformist wing. Though his carrot and stick tactic of using social reforms to draw the work-force away from revolutionary social democracy failed in the short term, the political identification of a large segment of labour with the Reich grew in the long term, especially after the Socialist Law was revoked in 1890.

For the German Question it became crucial that in the battle against international social democracy within the working class, one wing so identified with its own country that it fought for a nationally defined, one-nation socialism. As German *national* socialism, this wing stood against Marxist-oriented *international* socialism. The German NSDAP, shaped by the Austrian Pan-German and anti-Semite Adolf Hitler, later gave its own answer to the German Question: a *großdeutsch* Reich encompassing as many Germans as possible, without regard to the 'alien' minorities absorbed into the Reich, let alone Jews.

Consequences for foreign policy: from continental politics to *Weltpolitik*

The First World War swirled all these elements around as if in some global fiery furnace, producing new combinations which in turn determined Germany's path towards the Second World War and the subsequent new departure of the German Question in 1945. They may be summarized as the will to enhance German power – from continental power, to German *Weltpolitik* or 'world politics', to Germany's actual attempt to seize world-power status (*Griff nach der Weltmacht*) in the First World War, with the additional temptation of global domination being within her grasp.[13]

The *kleindeutsch* version of German unification was the only one that Europe could tolerate: Bismarck knew only too well that any attempt to exceed these limits would be fatal. But he neglected to educate the German nation about the disastrous consequences of more power for the Reich. After his fall in 1890, such insights were in short supply. On the contrary, blinded by 'vengeful opposition' (Thomas Nipperdey) to his hated successor Caprivi, Bismarck allied himself against his own better judgement with the Pan-Germans who were just beginning to surface. They reached beyond the relative self-restraint of what he had himself created towards the super-*großdeutsch* solution which would eventually destroy his Reich. Uninterrupted demographic and economic growth vastly increased the sensation of power and the desire to expand. The Reich felt hemmed in and aspired to an even 'greater Germany'.

Bismarck's continental policies, continued in modified form by his first successor Caprivi (1890–94), can be seen, broadly speaking, as the usual pause for consolidation of a new power centre, to enable it to digest the fruits of its new power. But the foundation of the Reich raised new problems: Austria and France had already been defeated. The two Great Powers flanking the European system, Russia and Great Britain, were threatened by being quantitatively outstripped and qualitatively outclassed by the growth of the German Reich.

In accordance with the normal mechanisms of classical power politics, Germany sought expansion along the path of least resistance. Austria-Hungary was the weakest link in the chain of European Great Powers; soon after 1871, Bismarck yielded to the temptation to divide up the weakened Austria-Hungary in a power-political arrangement between Germany and its traditional ally Russia. He discreetly indicated that Russia could have a free hand in the 'Orient' – the Balkans – i.e. against Austria-Hungary, if Russia agreed to leave Germany a free hand in the West so that she might once again defeat France, which had recovered surprisingly quickly after 1873. Russia rejected the offer, and, along with Britain, intervened to protest energetically in Berlin when Bismarck threatened France obliquely with 'preventive war' during the 'war-in-sight' crisis of April/May 1875.[14] That was effectively the end of one *großdeutsch* solution (though one reduced by those regions which were to have fallen to Russia) – a variant of the maxi-*großdeutsch* solution of 1848 – even though it was to resurface repeatedly in the speculations of diplomats right up to the eve of the First World War.

The other variant, expansion through Austria-Hungary, was indirect and more elegant: the Dual Alliance of Germany with Austria-Hungary in 1879 was the almost automatic consequence of the Great Oriental Crisis of 1875–78. Russia's veiled threats of war contained in the 'Slap in the face letter' of August 1879 forced the Reich to relinquish what Bismarck had hitherto regarded as the ideal constellation whereby no Great Power entered into a peacetime alliance. Now Germany had to seek an ally: Russia or Austria-Hungary. Alliance with Russia would have led to the dividing up of Austria-Hungary between Germany and Russia. But after the Great Oriental Crisis, Bismarck perceived behind the façade of Czarist autocracy the workings of social and national (Pan-Slav) revolution, which one day could threaten Germany, too.

Austria-Hungary, by contrast, appeared the more consistently conservative option – now weakened, perhaps, but on that account (so it seemed) all the more easily manipulated by the stronger partner. In memoranda to Kaiser Wilhelm I, which are still worth reading today, Bismarck set out and justified with a breath-taking historical breadth of perspective his reasons for choosing Austria-Hungary: an intimate alliance with Austria-Hungary founded on international law would amount to a modified continuation of the Old Reich or the German Confederation: Vienna is German, hence ethnically, culturally and emotionally closer to the German Reich than Russia. Bismarck cleverly appealed to the latent *großdeutsch* sentiments of 1848.[15] As to how things would progress from this point on, he left it for the future to take care of.

Weltpolitik as the German version of imperialism

When, after the departure of Bismarck and Caprivi, Germany opted for *Weltpolitik* from 1895/96 onwards, new opportunities did in fact present themselves for overseas expansion of power. In the age of imperialism, this was the German version of the general imperialist expansion, and it had a particularly explosive outcome on the world stage.[16] Bismarck's modest colonial protectorates in Black Africa and the South Seas created an initial momentum as early as 1884/85 for the colonial and global politics he was later obliged to accede to, however reluctantly, as a concession to influential and fashionable currents in public opinion.

The continuing weakness of the Ottoman Empire, under constant pressure from Russia's southward expansion, was a temptation after

1898 to more active expansion in the Middle East. Germany wanted to take over the Ottoman Empire by providing economic aid and increasing the traditional Prussian military support it had given since 1829. The German-dominated Baghdad Railway became the symbol as well as the most important instrument of German expansion in the Near East.[17] But without a broader territorial basis in the south east, the project remained hanging in the air. Thus, Austria-Hungary was becoming the great transit land on the way to the Orient. The more it disintegrated internally, the more it subsided behind its façade into a mere client state of the ever more powerful German Reich. Ideally, the Baghdad Railway would extend to Berlin and Hamburg – by way of Vienna, but also through Belgrade.

The one stumbling-block to the Berlin-Baghdad railway line directly controlled from Germany, and indirectly via Austria-Hungary, became little Serbia – since its military revolt in 1903, once again the most active exponent of the South Slav movement.[18] From that time onwards, Germany was forced to support Austria-Hungary at almost any price, and thereby found herself drawn into the Balkan labyrinth with its tangled web of overlapping and clashing sub-imperial nationalisms. The catastrophic dialectical link between the German Question and the South Slav Question was detonated by the assassination at Sarajevo, which led straight into the First World War.

There was one serious internal structural weakness in the German Reich which prevented it finding an ally for its imperialist global expansion in either of the peripheral European powers, Britain or Russia.[19] As Prussia had been in the Crimean War, so united Germany was internally divided and deadlocked between the industrializing part west of the Elbe and the predominantly agrarian part to the east. The *Ostelbien* of the Junkers still preferred to seek support from autocratic Russia, but even there a switch to industrialization had come about after the emancipation of the serfs in 1861, financed mainly by foreign credit and grain exports. Since then, cheaper Russian grain competed with the main produce of the Prussian Junkers, also grain, on the internal German market. After the world economic crisis of 1873, the agrarians east of the Elbe changed from being free-traders (for their exports) into protectionists. The protective agrarian tariff imposed in 1879 initially most directly affected Russia and its industrialization programme.

Industry west of the Elbe took its ideological cues from Britain. However, heavy industry in, especially, the Rhineland, Westphalia and the Saar, increasingly argued for industrial tariffs to protect it against British industry. Interests of both agriculture and industry were met by the agrarian and industrial protective tariff of 1879, which largely put the German Reich on a new internal and external footing. But pressure from German heavy industry for the construction of a modern battle fleet succeeded in alienating Great Britain to such an extent that all tentative steps towards Anglo-German understanding around 1900 finally foundered.

Germany did not want to emerge on the stage of world politics as junior partner to the world's greatest naval and colonial power, but rather as a great power in its own right, reliant on its own might. In its power politics, however, and militarily as well in the First World War, it was burdened with Austria-Hungary. This fact also explains why the German Reich behaved as it did during the July crisis of 1914: Austria-Hungary was simply the only ally on which the otherwise globally isolated Reich could still rely. There were power-political as well as strategic considerations involved in this continuing alliance with the Habsburg monarchy – broadening the continental glacis as a basis for imperialistic world politics, and Austria-Hungary's position as a gateway to the Balkans and the Ottoman Empire. In addition, underlying Greater German sentiments left the future open for power-political options of a quite different kind: there was certainly a machiavellian side to Germany's *Nibelungentreue vis-à-vis* Austria – her 'blood-brotherhood' or 'undying loyalty on the Danube' – in the great pre-war crises.

First World War, 1914–1918

The global crisis – 'the seminal catastrophe of our century' (George F. Kennan) – redealt all the cards. It had come about because of rivalry between the Great Powers – above all because of the German Reich's ambition to become a world power by expansion overseas and towards the Orient. The Baghdad railway and the building of a battle fleet were both outward symbols and the hard core of German global power politics. What Germany saw as her 'encirclement' – in reality, the self-imposed isolation and containment of the dynamic Reich by Britain – was its direct and logical consequence: the alliance between France and Russia in 1892/94, and understandings between Britain and France in 1904 (the *Entente Cordiale*) and Russia in 1907, creating the Triple Entente as a counter-coalition to the German-led Triple Alliance.

What finally set alight tensions which had been building up over the previous decades was the clash between Hungarian chauvinism and the South Slav national movement. Behind Hungary stood the German Reich, whose *Weltpolitik* pushed for both power-political and territorial expansion. The fear was well-grounded that an Austria-Hungary which remained passive under pressure from both the South Slav movement and Russian Pan-Slavism would eventually collapse, but its collapse at the end of a major war, especially if defeated, looked even more certain. It seemed as if the foresight of the Austrian statesmen in the Crimean War of 1854 had been ignored or forgotten by their successors after 28 June 1914.[20]

The First World War threw up the German Question afresh in many respects, in context with the Polish Question and South Slav Question, even the Irish Question. The Italian Question, with the Irredentists demanding 'redemption', was decisive for Italy's entry into the war in 1915/16 against its erstwhile partners in the Triple Alliance.

The German Question appeared in its most explosive form after the outbreak of war in the German war aims – both official and secret.[21] The Pan-Germans once again played a crucial part, their influence out of all proportion to their status as a tiny minority. Formally, they represented only the extreme right in the spectrum of German war aims, and were apparently offset by the extreme left (USPD, Spartacus) and the bourgeois pacifists. In reality, however, the logic of power politics was on the side of the Pan-Germans: it was their version of maxi-*Großdeutschland*, or even super-*Großdeutschland*, as an answer to the German Question, to which the future appeared to belong.

German war aims initially combined a relatively modest extension of the *kleindeutsch* Reich through direct annexations in the east (the 'Polish border strip'[22]) and the west (Liège, Longwy-Briey) with a variant on the *großdeutsch* solutions dressed up in terms of *Mitteleuropa* or Central Europe.[23] Again and again, German troops had to come to the aid of Austria-Hungary when she suffered a serious defeat, in part because some of her non-German, in particular Czech, troops were defecting to the Russians. At the same time, there developed among the troops of the German Reich in Galicia, Wolhynia, Siebenbürgen and the Baltic a kind of solidarity which was both Greater-German and Pan-German, for the war brought them into contact with isolated pockets of the German diaspora of which they had previously been virtually ignorant, in which the people spoke German and lived according to German traditions. Thus, German plans for *Mitteleuropa* were put on a totally new footing, based on the experience of soldiers at the front. As late as early March 1917, when the Russian Revolution opened up grandiose new vistas, Kurt Riezler was suggesting that German hegemony should be 'disguised' by focusing on *Mitteleuropa*, using the modern analogy of 'hidden majorities' in joint-stock companies: just as Prussia dominated the German Reich, so the Reich could dominate 'its *Mitteleuropa*'.[24]

Bethmann Hollweg's September Programme of 9 September 1914 and the Pan-Germans' parallel power-political plans bear witness to this combination of direct and indirect expansion of power through annexations and vassal states. One was a more veiled, the other an open version of a *Mitteleuropa* stretching from Hamburg, or even the North Cape, to the Persian Gulf. In both cases rapid victory over France was essential. Bethmann Hollweg's inclusion of the neutral Netherlands and the Scandinavian states in a German-dominated *Mitteleuropa* even incorporated elements of the Pan-German *membra disiecta* theory, also in its application to south-eastern Belgium which had once belonged to the Old Reich.

Looking eastward, a reduced Poland (under direct Austro-German or German rule) and the annexation of the Baltic provinces would have expanded the basis of German power. But up to 1918, it remained open whether direct annexation or German client states would be best. In the south east, analogous arrangements were envisaged for Bulgaria, allied with Germany since 1915; Romania, defeated in 1916; and the Ottoman Empire, which was to be modernized by Germany. Serbia and Montenegro were to go to Austria-Hungary. The heart of *Mitteleuropa* was to be the Dual Alliance, which the German Reich at the beginning of 1918 wanted to strengthen further through constitutional ties, ideally into a confederation between Germany and Austria-Hungary.

After the collapse of Czarist Russia in 1917, German war aims under Ludendorff acquired Alexandrian dimensions: Finland, the Ukraine, Georgia and Armenia as German protectorates. After the separate Peace of Brest-Litowsk on 3 March 1918, the super-*Großdeutschland* solution beckoned for several months as a *fata morgana*. Hitler's inflammatory, chauvinistic speeches after the November revolution of 1918 returned to this aim again and again, and he tried militarily to put it into effect during the Second World War.

Germany's war aims can be summarized as an attempt to achieve hegemony in Europe as a territorial basis for her struggle to become a world power. *Mitteleuropa* had its corollary in a German '*Mittel-afrika*' south of the Sahara, envisaged in no less generous dimensions. Germany's positioning to seize world-power status in the First World War might well be followed in the next generation by her attempt to seize real world domination – something Kurt Riezler, pupil of Max Weber and adviser to Bethmann Hollweg, dreamed of in his war diaries.[25] The new German power centre proved to be so powerful that it all but single-handedly fought its enemies on the continent of Europe to a stalemate, and was only forced into submission by the entry into the war of the USA.

The Russian October Revolution of 1917 and Wilson's Fourteen Point Plan of 8 January 1918 caused a shift in the historical perspectives: Lenin and Wilson called for the right to self-determination for all peoples, an appeal to which Germany, the apparent victor, had to pay at least lip service when attempting to annexe the Baltic Provinces. Representatives of the German barons in the old Estates assembly asked for the protection of the German Reich without so much as consulting their Latvian and Estonian subjects.

The Bolshevik variant on the right to self-determination for all peoples became the instrument of communist revolution up to the establishment of the *Imperium Sovieticum* on the ruins of the Czarist empire. Wilson's bourgeois variant was the guiding principle behind the post-war settlement of Versailles in 1919. The Germans occupied a precarious middle ground between Lenin and Wilson. While the German Reich remained powerful, the right to national self-determination served to conceal German claims to more power. After her defeat in November 1918, the right to national self-determination became a gangplank to salvage whatever could still be saved 'for the nation'. Last-minute parliamentarization of the Reich was a desperate attempt to look more streamlined and democratic internally after Wilson had rejected armistice talks with the Kaiser.

For the Germans, military collapse came like a bolt from the blue, for the German troops still imagined themselves – in the often-repeated phrase – 'in the heart of enemy territory'. In reality, the German western front on 9 November 1918 had been pushed back almost to the German border. In the east they were still deep in Russia, but strategically, the eastern army was in a state of limbo, for a disintegrating Austria-Hungary had been forced to agree to the Allies marching through its territory, if necessary, as part of her armistice agreement. By early 1919 at the latest, allied troops would have been able to march through the Tirol into Bavaria, through Bohemia into Saxony, and from there on to Berlin. The situation which applied on 8 May 1945 would have been reached in early 1919 – *debellatio*, the complete military subjugation of the Reich.

It should have been only too clear to anyone looking at the military maps of November 1918 that the 'stab-in-the-back' was from its inception a myth, a lie invented by those in the Reich responsible for the real débâcle, in order to divert attention – which, of course, it did.

The Russian October Revolution had an instant and direct effect on the German November Revolution of 1918, but this was *also* a classical case of a sudden collapse after a military defeat. Two seemingly opposing principles were in contention, but in their overall historical effect they complemented and completed one another. Those in charge of what was since 3 October 1918 a modified, parliamentary Reich, new faces as well as old, made desperate attempts from above to negotiate an armistice with the Allies in order to save the Reich as a politically sovereign entity. From below, however, the revolution simply wanted to terminate the war and employed a remarkable range of methods – from refusing to obey orders, to mutiny (in the navy) and a general strike of workers in or without uniform – if possible before the allied armies actually set foot on German soil.

Both of these pragmatic though unobtrusive aims were achieved: armistice was indeed declared, after the revolution had also reached Berlin, the capital of the Reich, on 9 November, with Germany's sovereignty unimpaired. The new central government was weak: the Provisional Government followed the Soviet model even in its official name, the *Rat der Volksbeauftragten*, but its chairman, the more conservative Social Democrat Friedrich Ebert, secretly relied on the old army command (OHL) under Groener and Hindenburg and crushed all efforts by the new left – from the Communist KPD to the leftist USPD – to turn the German collapse after defeat into a true Communist revolution to join world revolution à la Lenin.

REPUBLICAN INTERREGNUM, 1918–1933

Wedged in between the Second and the Third Reichs – in its substance as well as its chronology – the Weimar Republic never really had a chance to become properly established. As the unloved child of military defeat, it had to take the blame for what others had done before. Yet most Germans held their unpopular republic (one which lacked republicans – at least, in sufficient numbers) responsible for the (normal) consequences of defeat – chaos within and economic decline, culminating in hyperinflation, and externally for Versailles with its harsh consequences for Germany. After a short period of economic recovery and political stabilization, the world economic crisis of 1929 finished the Weimar Republic off.[26]

The 1918 November Revolution and Versailles

After the enormous exertions of the First World War, the German November Revolution of 1918 was an internal crisis of exhaustion and collapse, such as heavy defeats normally bring in their wake. Both 'Spartacus' and the newly-founded KPD attempted to extend the communist revolution on the Bolshevik model. And yet, in the subsequent

confusion of civil war-like proportions right up to the end of the hyperinflation in the autumn of 1923, the Reich neverthless remained intact
and sovereign. The Weimar Republic retained the federal structure of
the Reich, with Prussia continuing to occupy the strongest position,
under SPD leadership up to July 1932.

As if to compensate for the social revolution *manqué* of 1918/19, over
the next few years the SPD implemented the next stage in the development of Bismarck's social policies. But whereas Bismarck had created
them in order to provide social support for the monarchy, the new social
laws, in particular those governing works committees and unemployment insurance, were to buy the loyalty at least of the working class
towards the friendless Weimar Republic – whether or not this was the
intention, it was certainly the effect. While still in crisis after having lost
the war, Germany indulged in an even more costly social system, which
far exceeded what was economically possible at the time. It was not
surprising that the last parliamentary government – an SPD-led one –
collapsed at the end of March 1930, only months after the start of the
world economic crisis in October 1929, over its inability to finance
unemployment benefits in the face of steeply rising unemployment – the
fever chart of the Republic in its death throes.

The next major burden was imposed from without, by the Treaty of
Versailles. With boundaries redrawn, the question once again was: what
belongs to Germany? As expected, Germany lost its predominantly
non-German border regions (Alsace-Lorraine, Eupen-Malmedy,
northern Schleswig, Posen/Posnan-West Prussia, the eastern part of
Upper Silesia), but also predominantly German-populated Danzig,
which became a free city. More drastic French plans to weaken Germany further through 'Separatism' (turning its territories on the Rhine,
the Palatinate and Saarland into client states dependent on France)
were thwarted by Britain, which wanted to keep Germany intact as
a buffer zone against Russian bolshevism, quite apart from strong
German opposition. The Weimar Republic's loss of territory, her renun-
ciation of heavy armaments and general conscription, as well as
the internal conflicts which normally follow any heavy military defeat,
initially made her a relative power vacuum, virtually incapable of action
externally, though she was always able to maintain internal sovereignty.

By way of compensation for these losses, there appeared briefly on
the political horizon the most modest form of the Pan-German solution, the 'mini-*Großdeutschland*' variant to which those *Reichsdeutsche*
(as they would later be called) in the Frankfurt Paulskirche in 1848 had
demanded the German Austrians accede: the German Austrians and
the *Sudetendeutsche* living on the borders of Bohemia and Moravia

claimed their right to self-determination through *Anschluss* with the Weimar Republic. The Austrians saw no future for a small Austria consisting of a German rump, with its capital, once the capital of a major dynastic state, situated on its eastern border. Still less did the Sudeten Germans wish to be a minority on the periphery of a new Czechoslovakia which embraced lands of the Wenceslas Crown, including those regions on the borders with Germany which had mainly German inhabitants.

However, the logic of power appeared somewhat different, though no less obvious, to the Allies: Germany strengthened by the *Anschluss* with German Austria and the Sudetenland would have emerged once again as the strongest power in Europe. German hegemony would be permanently established, especially since she would become more nationally homogeneous than ever before after giving up her non-German border regions. In order to prevent this, the Allies expressly prohibited *Anschluß* in the Treaty of Versailles and in the peace treaties with Austria and Hungary. Austria was forced to become an independent state, like it or not, while the Sudeten Germans had to come to terms with the Czechs who were now the main nationality in the new Czechoslovakia. The Greater German option was blocked by international law.

The Treaty of Versailles was mild compared with the German war aims, with Brest-Litowsk in 1918[27] and Yalta/Potsdam in 1945. Yet it rankled in the collective consciousness of the nation, and most Germans felt its dictates to be discriminatory and unwarranted. These included War Guilt Clause 231; a prohibition on general conscription, a general staff and heavy armaments on land, sea and in the air; loss of western and eastern territories, in particular Danzig and the Polish Corridor; loss of colonies; reparations; prohibition on *Anschluß*; and prolonged occupation of the left bank of the Rhine.

It was the prohibition on *Anschluß* in particular which most Germans bitterly resented. They insisted on their right to self-determination without considering, let alone accepting, the legitimate power-political calculations of the Allies. The great majority of Germans remained blind to the explosive situation which *Großdeutschland's* unification as a nation-state in the middle of Europe would have created: after the First World War, quantitatively the second largest people in Europe was still qualitatively the strongest on the continent. That is what the French prime minister Clemenceau meant during the Paris Peace Conference when he sighed that the situation would have been be very different 'if there were 20 million fewer Germans in the middle of Europe' – a phrase subsequently twisted by German nationalistic propaganda.

Clemenceau was not invoking genocide, but merely his despair at the insolubility of the German Question: in terms of power politics, it would have been easier to cope with 60 million Germans at the heart of Europe than 80 million.

The Weimar Republic, 1919–1933

By 1924, after it had overcome inflation in 1923 and again achieved stability, with the rentenmark and the Dawes Plan regulating its reparation payments and access to foreign loans (mainly from the USA), it rapidly became clear that Germany was still a latent European Great Power: once the Reich had fully recovered, its power-political position would be even stronger in relative terms than before the First World War. The disintegration of the Habsburg monarchy and Russia's transformation into a revolutionary state left a power vacuum to the east of *Mitteleuropa* and in south-eastern Europe which the successor states were too weak, heterogeneous, internally divided and mutually antagonistic to fill by themselves. Russia had been marginalized and was now distant and isolated from Europe, mainly because of the newly reconstituted Poland, albeit a Poland which had not been able to regain the historical borders of 1772 to which it aspired.

The First World War had taken a bloody toll on France, with Verdun the traumatic symbol of its war-weariness and general exhaustion. It did indeed attempt to compensate for the Russian alliance which it had lost in the October Revolution, through the 'Cordon Sanitaire' and the Little Entente, but in so doing asked too much of the successor states between Germany and Soviet Russia. They were to protect Europe from communism while keeping Germany and Russia apart, but at the same time, as members of the alliance behind Germany's back, keep the Reich in check.

The foreign policy of the Weimar Republic[28] was even more caught up in the tension between West and East than had been that of the Second Reich. The Russian October Revolution modified both the European system as a whole and Germany's position within it. Lenin's strategy of world revolution assumed that Germany, with both its industry and its socialism highly developed, would be the revolution's first conquest, if necessary by military means via Poland. 'Berlin, here we come!' was the Red Army's real agenda in the Polish-Soviet war of 1920/21.

The German Question had now aquired a new twist: would the Reich, having been defeated and humiliated by the West, join the communist world revolution against the victors out of sheer spite? This is what the Allies feared after Rapallo in 1922. But the victory of the

Polish troops under Marshal Pilsudski in August 1920 – the Poles' 'miracle on the Vistula' – later forced Soviet Russia to pursue 'Socialism in one country' (Stalin) instead. It thus saved the Germans of the Weimar Republic from having to declare their allegiance and make an open choice between joining the world revolution (out of *schadenfreude* that Poland would then disappear once more), or throwing in their lot with the equally detested Allies.

It is possible that the Red Army's advance to the borders of East Prussia had a further effect. In the plebiscite of 1920 to decide whether southern East Prussia should become Polish, or remain German, the overwhelming majority – also of the Masurian, i.e. non-German-speaking population – voted for Germany. After 1945, the Poles interpreted this vote as an instance of specific historical circumstances swaying public opinion. The result was said to have been an expression of the Masurian preference for the stability offered by the larger Germany to the communism which was advancing from the east and which had already half-overrun Poland.

Just as every defeated major power had attempted to do after heavy defeat at the hands of a European coalition – France in 1713/14 and 1815, Russia in 1856 and 1917/18 – the Germany of the Weimar Republic sought to revise the international regime imposed upon it, in this case at Versailles. After consolidation through the ending of hyperinflation late in 1923 and the scaling-down of reparations, including US loans, thanks to the Dawes Plan in 1924, the next short-term goal was the formal recognition of the Reich as a major European power again.

Only in the Locarno treaties of 1925 did the Weimar Republic's status as a major European power receive recognition. Under Foreign Minister Gustav Stresemann (1923–29), Germany solemnly recognized its western borders with France (Alsace-Lorraine) and Belgium (Eupen-Malmedy). In return, the French forces of occupation withdrew from the western territories of the Reich before the date set at Versailles, and Germany was admitted to the League of Nations in 1926 and given the status of Permanent Member of the Council of the League – a privilege otherwise granted only to Great Powers.

In recognition of her exposed position and to reward her for her (partial) commitment to the West at Locarno, Britain and France permitted the Weimar Republic to develop her special relationship with Russia after Rapallo in 1922, by the Treaty of Berlin of 1926. Germany was not automatically obliged to participate in a war of the League of Nations against Soviet Russia in defence of Poland, but retained a free hand to decide, in accordance with her 'national' interests. These were to be determined by her front-line position *vis-à-vis* the unloved 'seasonal state' of Poland – a position Germany shared with the Soviet Union – and by secret cooperation between the Red Army and the *Reichswehr* which enabled Germany to circumvent the Treaty of Versailles and develop and test prohibited heavy armaments in remote areas of the Soviet Union. In exchange, Soviet officers were initiated in the deeper mysteries of the art of war by the *Truppenamt* (the General Staff in all but name), knowledge which they successfully employed against the Third Reich during the Second World War.

The common German-Soviet goal of pushing Poland back to its 'ethnic frontiers' once again raised the explosive issue of the border as part of the German Question. What should belong to Germany? While recognizing the new borders in the West in 1925, the Weimar Republic had firmly rejected Poland's and Czechoslovakia's demands for a parallel 'Eastern Locarno'.[29] Consequently, she reserved the right to revise the eastern borders of 1919 when the opportunity arose. West Prussia and Danzig, the Polish Corridor, which since Versailles had isolated East Prussia from the rest of the Reich, became part of the web of German aspirations directed against Poland.

At least in retrospect, Germany's refusal to contemplate an 'Eastern Locarno' can be seen as prefiguring the Hitler-Stalin Pact – effectively the opening move of the Second World War, completing the destruction of the Versailles settlement.

During the death throes of the Weimar Republic, the German Question arose in several quite distinctive forms, both internally and externally. The secret 'Black *Reichswehr*' was to support the official *Reichswehr* in any conflict with Poland, whose army was still superior to that of the Reich. The murder of Potempa in Upper Silesia in 1932 openly linked the ideological battle against communism with the ethnic struggle against Poland. The SA men's victim was a Polish-speaking communist – Hitler's declaration of solidarity with the perpetrators was as dramatic as it was cynical.

In general, the Weimar Republic kept open the possibility of renewed expansion beyond the borders imposed at Versailles: the *Auswärtiges Amt* secretly financed, coordinated and organized the 'campaign against the lie that Germany was responsible for the War', while demands were made for a revision of the eastern borders. From its beginnings in the November Revolution of 1918, the Weimar Republic had in general drifted almost continuously from Left (the Council of Representatives of the People made up of USPD and SPD) to far Right (Hitler and the NSDAP), apart from the two grand coalitions with SPD participation (1923) and under SPD leadership (1928–30).

The Great Slump of 1929 dramatically accelerated this rightward shift, with a succession of presidential-style governments from early 1930 onwards under Brüning, Papen, Schleicher and Hitler eroding the parliamentary republic. The Weimar Republic was crushed between the two polarized totalitarian parties of the extreme left (KPD) and the extreme right (NSDAP) – the latter becoming the strongest party in the Reich and most of the *länder* in 1932. Together, these parties formed a negative absolute majority in the Reichstag which paralysed all governments.

The world economic crisis begining in 1929 gave rise everywhere to serious political crises, especially at its height (or depth) in 1931 – in Great Britain, South Africa, Chile, New Zealand. In Europe it made possible the authoritarian Dollfuss regime; it radicalized monarchist and presidential dictatorships, fascism in Italy and communism in the Soviet Union; in the USA it sealed the fate of the Republican Hoover and in Japan it led to the replacement of formal party rule by an almost open military dictatorship. The particularly extreme reaction to it in Germany can be explained by her heavy defeat in the First World War and the crises which followed – revolution, chaos and hyperinflation up to 1923 – which had a cumulative traumatic effect. Under the impact of the world economic crisis and faced with the KPD's growing threat of an extreme-Left, international-socialist Soviet Germany bent on joining Soviet Russia, the Germans collapsed for a second time, this time politically towards the extreme Right and into the national socialist Third Reich, which by contrast seemed to stand for and to promise a continuity of German traditions.

In a desperate search for some success, at least in foreign policy, Brüning launched the idea of a customs union with Austria in 1931, which would have given the Reich new economic momentum (with an enlarged German market) and a psychological boost politically. But France (rightly) suspected that the customs union project was merely a first step to outright *Anschluß* with Austria in the medium term, and immediately called a halt to the project, drawing attention to the prohibition on *Anschluß* in the Treaty of Versailles. The Weimar Republic had to continue stewing in its own *kleindeutsch* juice, up to the bitter end in 1933, which, by one of the ironies of history, an Austrian as German Chancellor was preparing for it – one to whom only five years later the anxious world powers were even ready to concede open *Anschluß* with Austria and the Sudetenland – the mini-*Großdeutschland* solution of 1848 and 1918/19 now carried the day under threat of military invasion of the German (henceforth Greater German) *Wehrmacht*.

THIRD REICH AND SECOND WORLD WAR, 1933–1945

The external German Question: revision and expansion

The main reason for the victory of National Socialism in the final stages of the *kleindeutsch* Reich of the Weimar Republic was the Germans' sense of uncertainty and insecurity regarding their position in Europe and the world. In 1871 the German Question seemed to have been definitively settled, but it had been violently thrown up anew in 1918/19 by the express desire of the German Austrians and the Sudeten Germans in Bohemia and Moravia for *Anschluß* with the Reich, and it was now directed at the Germans themselves. What did they want to be in Europe? One nation among others within a system which had hitherto always resisted the hegemony of any single European power? Or was defeat in 1918, at the hands of almost the whole world, merely an incentive to do better next time?

What Hitler and the NSDAP were agitating for, which was borne out by the subsequent course of history up to 1939 and 1945, shows that most Germans preferred the second alternative. The circumstances of Germany's geographical position in Europe, the more onerous stipulations of the Treaty of Versailles, the political weakness of her neighbours to the east and the south east – all helped bring about a programme of German revisionism. Hitler merely took over from the Weimar Republic and carried it out, effecting a smooth transition from the limited revisionism of wanting to return to the borders of 1914, to running amok in a Greater German crusade against Europe and the world.

The logic of geography, of the patterns of domestic and foreign policy and of traditional power politics, all combined to produce a sequence of coordinated steps which any bright German schoolchild of the day could reel off: first, political unity and internal consolidation, then external expansion. Hitler achieved internal unity in his centralized, one-party/one-leader state in 1933/34 by a combination of meek compliance and sheer terror, disguised by clever propaganda. At least for members of the German *Volk*, the bureaucratic state based on the rule of law continued – with limitations – as before, though its source of legitimacy was new: 'The *Führer* protects the law' (Carl Schmitt).

The traditional momentum of (ostensible) success and terror quashed all serious resistance to an expansionary programme which sought to remove the alleged 'injustice' of the '*Diktat*' or 'shameful peace' of Versailles. Resentment at being 'deprived of the right to self-determination' was uppermost in people's minds. By sweeping aside the clause of the Versailles Treaty prohibiting *Anschluß*, Hitler in March 1938 fulfilled the 1848 national dream of a Greater German answer to the German Question.

The internal German Question: who is German?

The Third Reich, like the Second Reich, promptly raised again the internal aspect of the German Question in 1933: Who is German? Who has a right to call himself a German? The Third Reich began by suppressing any dissent normal in a modern industrialized society, by forcing it underground or into exile. Under National Socialism, concentration camps and exile were logical consequences of the question Bismarck had been the first to ask: Who are the enemies of the Reich? At first it was primarily Marxists – Social Democrats and Communists – who were sent to the camps, then 'bourgeois' democrats, mainly from the Catholic Centre party. Following the victory of the NSDAP, anti-Semitism, hitherto the preserve of the extreme Right, became the official doctrine of the Reich. Jews, too, could not (any longer) be Germans. During the war, the mentally ill were 'eradicated' in the euthanasia programme, followed by the gypsies (Sinti, Roma), as a preliminary to the 'Final Solution'.

By pushing into exile academics and artists with democratic convictions, often of Jewish origin, the Third Reich brought to an abrupt end the wide prestige of German universities since 1810, German culture and German science. Academic emigrés in turn enriched and strengthened the potential of their newly adopted host countries. To mention only one representative example: Albert Einstein and a group of leading atomic physicists in the USA built America's atom bomb, the 'Manhattan Project', begun in 1942, to pre-empt what was thought to be the serious threat of a German atom bomb. Those who remained were used by the Nazi regime to help construct their war machine with frightful efficiency and for propaganda purposes in the service of the Third Reich, in the name of those cultural values which the regime had betrayed. Yet even this intellectual and scientific rump was sufficient to create so formidable a war machine that it was only finally defeated in the Second World War by the united strength of almost every other nation.

Revision and gradual expansion, 1933–1939

A high price was paid for the enforced eradication and suppression of dissent in the Third Reich: internal tensions, unable to surface, found an outlet in aggression towards the outside world. Almost the only remaining serious differences of opinion within the Nazi regime were about the goals and methods of expansion. A return to the borders of 1914 plus *Anschluß* with Austria and the Sudetenland would have given the Germans no more than their 'right to self-determination' (an argument still frequently heard after 1945). 'Revision' of Versailles and its borders – in reality, the overthrow of the system itself – quickly escalated into demands for further conquests.

After internal unity had been achieved under duress, the logical next step was to recover external freedom of action and thereby full sovereignty. Hitler used the necessary period of consolidation to negotiate the Concordat of 20 July 1933 with the Vatican – a foreign policy move which helped to complete his one-party state at home by neutralizing the Catholic *Zentrum* party. By withdrawing from the League of Nations in November 1933, the intention was to remove moral scruples as well as objections to German rearmament in international law, for it was the complex question of disarmament which Hitler used as a pretext for leaving the unloved League.

After that, the non-aggression pact with Poland in January 1934 was Hitler's first genuine success in foreign policy: Poland, with its authoritarian regime, was virtually eliminated as an ally of France, becoming instead a secret ally of the Reich. The plebiscite in the Saarland in January 1935 had been decided upon long before 1933, but it was to be the first triumph of Hitler's regime, again combining home with foreign policy. Now the Saarland had returned '*heim ins Reich*', its population and economic strength also increased the Third Reich's military potential.

Deliberate infringements of the Treaty of Versailles subsequently marked its unilateral rejection: the next steps were the reintroduction of universal conscription in 1935 and the occupation of the Rhineland in 1936. France and Britain did nothing ('appeasement'), for they had still not recovered from the First World War and were keen to avoid another war with Germany. Germany's unofficial military intervention (the 'Condor Legion') in support of Franco in the Spanish Civil War of 1936–39, alongside Fascist Italy, consolidated an ideological alliance, while allowing modern weapons to be tested under conditions of war and the coordinated operations of ground and airborne troops. The bombing of Guernica in 1937 was perhaps the first deliberate use of terror from the air.

The impulse towards a Greater Germany remained latent and found its logical outcome in the *Anschluß* with Austria in March 1938, followed by the annexation of the Sudetenland in October 1938. What was henceforth officially known as the Greater German Reich openly enjoyed European hegemony: Austria gave it access to the Balkans, where most states now looked for orientation to the Reich with its increased power. The Third Reich now also bordered directly on its ideological neighbour, Fascist Italy. Occupation of the rest of Czecho-slovakia and the establishment of the Protectorate of Bohemia and Moravia on 15 March 1939, reversed Palacky's rejection of the Frank-furt Paulskirche Parliament in 1848. The Czechs, who since the destruc-tion of the Greater Moravian Empire by the Hungarians in 907 had been heavily dependent on the more powerful Germans, became second-class citizens of the Reich, endowed with only a rudimentary internal autonomy. The forced reintegration of the Memelland region of Lithuania on 22 March 1939 was Hitler's last 'peaceful' foreign policy success, completing the base from which subsequent campaigns of conquest would be launched.

Poland and the outbreak of war, 1939

Hitler's next objective was Poland, the 'seasonal state' hated by Ger-many and Russia alike. Even Hitler did not want a Second World War. What he wanted was to continue his limited acts of aggression against weak opponents in isolation, if possible by political and diplomatic means, if necessary by military force. As late as 1938, Poland had refused to participate in a German anti-Bolshevist 'crusade' against the Soviet Union, fearful of being crushed between the two totalitarian powers: if the Germans won, they would reduce Poland to a client state of Germany; if the Soviets won, they would impose the communist revolution on Poland. Wedged between neighbours whose power had grown, and geographically cut off from the West by Germany, Poland seemed to offer Hitler the ideal next step, after Prague and the Memel-land, towards conquest by bullying or a localized war.

But by occupying Prague, Hitler had finally pushed Britain beyond the limit of what she could tolerate. Poland being the obvious next objective for German expansion, on 31 March 1939, Britain declared that she would guarantee Polish independence – a guarantee which Hitler sought to undermine with the Hitler-Stalin Pact of 23 August 1939. This non-aggression pact, with its secret additional protocol carv-ing up eastern *Mitteleuropa* between Greater Germany and the USSR, was a further example of German-Russian collaboration against Poland, a tradition stretching back to the partitions of Poland. Hitler wanted to localize the conflict and keep a free hand in his dealings with Poland, even if it meant allowing Stalin huge territorial gains: Eastern

Poland, the Baltic states in 1939/40, Romanian Bessarabia (now Moldavia) in 1940. Since Poland did not accede to the seemingly modest German demands (Danzig, exterritorial railway and autobahn through the Polish Corridor) – demands which in reality would have reduced her to a satellite of Germany – on 1 September 1939 Hitler gave orders for the long-planned invasion of Poland.

Second World War, 1939–1945, and 'Final Solution', 1941–1945

Britain and France's declaration of war on 3 September 1939 was seen by Hitler and his closest associates as a catastrophe: Hitler's strategy of local acts of aggression below the threshold of general war had broken down. The spectre of defeat haunted the leaders of the Reich from the very first day of the Second World War.

Germany's next military objectives were a logical outcome of the war situation. In the West, while the Allies staged their 'phoney war', this remained largely formal and passive. France fell in May/June 1940, but in the Battle of Britain, Great Britain successfully warded off what was intended as the preparatory stage of a German invasion ('Operation Sea Lion'). Nevertheless, the series of blitzkrieg campaigns and victories against isolated and technically or numerically inferior or internally demoralized enemies in 1940 created a base from which to attack the real ideological and power-political enemy: the communist Soviet Union. Victory over 'Bolshevism' would simultaneously open up wider scope for 'the people without space' (*Volk ohne Raum*).

At first, Stalin's Soviet Union was shaken by the thrust of the German offensive in the summer and autumn of 1941, and its inherent weakness as a left-wing totalitarian state even threatened to pull the country apart. But the way the Germans waged war against 'subhuman' Slavs and Jews proved even more cruel than the Stalinist regime, allowing him to mobilize patriotic and anti-fascist sentiment in defence of the country against the German aggressors. Russian recovery was assisted by a non-aggression pact with Japan, massive US loans and material aid after Pearl Harbor, followed by Hitler's declaration of war against the USA on 11 December 1941. When the German Sixth Army was encircled at Stalingrad in November 1942 and Rommel's *Afrikakorps* was thrown back at El Alamein, the initiative passed to the Allies.

The industrial potential and technical know-how accumulated in Germany since 1800 had erupted for a second time within twenty-five years in simultaneous aggression against West and East. At the height of its power, which by the end of 1942 extended from the Atlantic seaboard in the west, as far as Stalingrad in the east and El Alamein in the south-east, a super-*Großdeutschland* awed the world, combining extensive direct annexations, protectorates, provinces and satellite states.

Even before this conquest had been achieved, the 'Final Solution of the Jewish Question' through mass murder was under way, as predicted as long ago as 1881 by a left-wing liberal worried by the first signs of anti-Semitism among *reichsdeutsch* 'patriots'. Among the minorities which found themselves under Greater German rule were the mainly Ashkenazim Jews whose ancestors in 1349 had found refuge in Poland from pogroms, especially those of the German flagellants. These now became the main victims of the Holocaust.

With the Holocaust, Hitler's super-*Großdeutschland* solution took on a new dimension, far transcending both Germany and Europe. To the global crime of the Second World War, the Third Reich added the global crime of 'Auschwitz', thereby finally linking the German Question with the Jewish Question. In his battle against Bolshevism, linked as it was for the Nazi regime with the Jewish Question by way of the 'Jewish-Bolshevist world conspiracy', Hitler was simultaneously attacking his other 'global enemy', the Jews. The right-wing totalitarian, secularized fundamentalism of German National Socialism claimed the right to annihilate the left-wing totalitarian, secularized fundamentalism of Russian International Socialism *and* 'international world Jewry' in the name of humanity itself: the Waffen SS, massively expanded after 1939, professed to represent anti-communist Europe. Just as *Mitteleuropa* in the First World War had been a cover for German hegemony in Europe, so the SS now propagated their own 'Greater Germanic Reich of the German Nation' as self-appointed custodians of Europe.

As in the First World War, it was the USA, the last of the major powers to remain neutral, which turned the scales decisively against Germany. Global resistance to Germany's war aims and Hitler's concept of 'total war' led to the Allies' demand for Germany's unconditional surrender, as a way of depriving her once and for all of the means to seek revenge ever again. If necessary, the total capitulation of the Greater German Reich would have been enforced by use of the Second World War's most deadly weapon: the first two atom bombs had originally been intended for Germany – for Berlin and Frankfurt am Main. It was only because Germany surrendered more quickly, on 8 May 1945, than the Allies had feared might have been the case, that the bombs were dropped instead on Hiroshima and Nagasaki.

4 Germany as a power vacuum
Division, 1945–1989/90

The ending of the Third Reich plunged the Germans into a state of tension between liberation from National Socialism and 'collapse' – *Zusammenbruch* was the term most Germans had begun to use again for the end of the war. At the same time, the dialectics of defeat, denazification, the division of the country and a fresh political start, unleashed a dynamism which, through the logic of the Cold War and the different economic systems in East and West, nevertheless resulted eventually in the reunification of Germany, in 1990. After 1945, it was the division of Germany, and how to overcome it, which was thought to constitute the German Question. Seen from an historical perspective, with Germany divided by the Cold War, all roads led to Berlin after all.

But at first, defeated and divided Germany was again a power vacuum. What power it regained in the context of the Cold War was neutralized from 1949 onwards in two German states, autonomous at first, then with limited sovereignty after 1955. As members of ideologically opposed global blocs, they confronted each other in a new German dualism. Unlike the first German dualism of Austria and Prussia (1740–1866), however, the confrontation was not between North and South, but between East and West, with its boundary on the rivers Elbe and Saale, roughly the boundaries of 800 and 1492/98.

GERMANY UNDER OCCUPATION, 1945–1949

The German supernova had exploded in May 1945. The new power vacuum was filled by the victors of the Second World War as occupying powers. But the peace treaty, originally intended to have followed the model of Versailles in 1919, became a victim of the Cold War.

Point of departure: end of the Reich and a new political start, May 1945

Unconditional surrender by the Greater German *Wehrmacht* on 8 May 1945 brought the Second World War to a close for the Germans and gave them the opportunity to begin afresh politically. Whereas the *Kaiserreich* had narrowly avoided total military defeat by its timely armistice before the outbreak of the November Revolution in 1918, total military defeat is what occurred in May 1945. At the end of the war, Germany lost her statehood and sovereignty in international law. This was outwardly enacted and symbolized by the dissolution and imprisonment of the last government of the Reich under Dönitz on 23 May 1945. Henceforth, the German Question took on yet another new form: how can the Germans be organized in such a way that they are no longer dangerous, but are still reasonably satisfied?

Unconditional surrender meant that sovereignty in Germany passed to the victorious Allies, represented and exercised by the three, subsequently four, occupying powers – the USA, the USSR, Britain and France. The German power vacuum was filled in terms of international law by a condominium of the four occupying powers. They put it under the control of their military governments in four zones of occupation, authorizing political involvement in various degrees and forms as democratic parties and trade unions emerged and were officially recognized. This new political beginning was marked by participation, first at the lowest level of local administration, then at the level of the *Länder*, and finally, in 1949, in a Germany which was already divided, at the highest level. The gradual relaxation of control by the occupying powers – in the West more than in the East – was matched by the growth of internal autonomy to near-sovereignty.

World-historical context: the Cold War and its conclusion, 1945–1990

Inevitably, the democratic western occupying powers and the Stalinist Soviet Union left their mark on their respective occupation zones. But the Soviet Union's subjection of the peoples of east and south-east Europe to communist rule as new buffer states between Russia and Germany was contrary to what had been agreed. Henceforth, German answers to the chronic German Question were fused into issues connected with the Cold War: with the partition of Europe, the new global structural divide ran through the middle of Germany and Berlin.

In the Cold War it was the Germans, on both sides of the Iron Curtain, who were more intensely involved than any other people in divided Europe. They soon rose to become the star pupils of their respective controlling powers, and the next most important players of the two camps. At the same time, the traditional question concerning Germany's place between East and West took on a new dimension: because it had never been able, for structural reasons, to decide unequivocally between East and West, once Russia assumed a position of hegemony in eastern Europe, Germany was split between the liberal, democratic West and the communist, totalitarian East. Global political rivalry during the Cold War governed the future course of divided Germany.

On the other hand, the Cold War was only the most recent example of a situation familiar throughout history: coalitions soon break up after the common enemy has been defeated. The 'anti-Hitler coalition' – an emotive term used by communists and their fellow travellers in particular to describe the alliance of opposites formed with this one specific purpose in mind – duly collapsed immediately after the Second World War. There could be no permanent bond, for the belief in democracy which both sides formally professed, in practice meant something very different in either case. For the West, Stalin's Soviet communism was a real threat to the extent that Stalin was seemingly attempting to keep up the momentum, even beyond the Elbe, of communism's westward expansion in pursuit of the defeated Third Reich.

As a conflict between East and West, the Cold War combined a contest between two global ideological systems with power-political rivalry between two superpowers. Of the major powers competing for supremacy up to 1945, these two remained, and they were now competing for world domination. Between them lay Germany, which, on account of her strategic position in the middle of Europe and the considerable intellectual and economic potential she retained even in 1945, neither side was willing to yield to the other without a fight. It was not by chance that the Cold War began with the collapse and *de facto* division of Germany in May 1945, and that it ended when this division was removed by the collapse of the Berlin Wall on 9 November 1989.

This 'ideological contest', as it was generally called in the early 1960s, created the global context for Germany's political development, which in turn also influenced the Cold War and its consequences. Conversely, politics in and around Germany after 1945 cannot be understood without reference to the general global trend – the rise and fall of communism.

In formal terms, Germany's changing status in the world can be gauged by her relations with the UN: like the League of Nations after the First World War, the United Nations initially came into being as a permanent political alliance of the Allied powers to secure the peace against Germany – as can be seen in the UN clause dealing with enemy states. It was only in the transition from *de facto* recognition of the division of Germany, and subsequent acceptance of both German states into the UN in 1972, to German unity in 1990, that the United Nations became a truly universal organization. After German unification in 1990 and Japan's elevation to membership of the UN Security Council in 1991, Germany's membership of the Security Council inevitably became an issue as well.

Germany as power vacuum: between continuities and new beginning

In May 1945, Germany lay prostrate before the superpowers, their allies (in the West) and satellites (in the East), largely in ruins, inundated by refugees from the east and the south-east whose return *heim ins Reich* was proving very different from the incorporation of their homelands in a Greater Germany which Hitler's slogan had promised. Territorially, Germany had undergone amputation compared with 1937, let alone with the Greater German Reich at its peak in 1941/42: Austria's independence was restored, the Sudetenland was returned to Czechoslovakia; while Alsace-Lorraine, Eupen-Malmedy and northern Schleswig, whose status had in each case been indeterminate (neither annexation nor autonomy) during the Third Reich, reverted to France, Belgium and Denmark respectively; in addition, some villages were given to the Netherlands, and parts of Slovenia, which had been annexed as late as 1944, to Yugoslavia. Poland regained Danzig, Posen/Posnan, West Prussia and eastern Upper Silesia, and won the territories to the east of the Oder-Neisse line including most of Silesia plus southern and western East Prussia, while north-eastern East Prussia around Königsberg and the Memelland went to the Soviet Union. Germany retained only the German heartland between the Rhine and the Oder, which was in turn subdivided into four occupation zones. Now it was up to the Allies to answer what was once again, after 1945, the open German Question.

The Cold War meant an unequivocal answer was impossible, for at its outset the dissolution of the 'anti-Hitler coalition' gave the Germans new scope: both sides in the Cold War wanted to get 'their' Germans on their side, so that they could win at least moral victories over the other part of Germany. It was only during this immediate post-war period that one hitherto unsatisfactory definition of the German Question became at least partially accurate: 'Who do the Germans belong to?' (Michael Stürmer): the democratic West or the communist East?

In many respects, 1945 really was 'year zero', a new starting point for the Germans, East and West, as the nation divided. Yet there were some elements of continuity: at first, the Germans found it difficult to think of themselves as no longer part of the Bismarckian Reich to which they had become accustomed as the model or norm for their national existence. For a variety of reasons, ghostly echoes of the Reich still cropped up here and there in both German states – in the Federal Republic there was 'Berlin, former capital of the *Reich*'; in the GDR there was the 'German Imperial Railway' (*Deutsche Reichsbahn*), still including MITROPA ('Middle European Sleeping Car Company'), a name going back to the opening of the railway line from Berlin to Constantinople, which had been controlled solely by the German Reich after the defeat of Serbia in 1915. But apart from such instances of patriotic nostalgia for the Reich, the transition from Reich to Federal Republic, or from Reich to GDR, was swift and (in the West more so than in the East) relatively unproblematic.

Among the most visible signs of continuity, especially in the West, were the churches, the trade unions, the economy and the political parties of the Weimar Republic (excluding the NSDAP, of course). In highly industrialized Germany, it was above all the material and intellectual infrastructure which survived. Although outwardly all appeared to have been destroyed, especially in the cities, infrastructures such as gas, water and telephone installations, roads and railways were still largely intact. After the radical proposals of the Morgenthau Plan to de-industrialize Germany were quickly scrapped, reconstruction commenced, this being the only way Germany could make reparations towards the reconstruction of the rest of Europe. Consequently, the 'ideological contest' became a question of which global system would reconstruct Germany more quickly, more efficiently and more humanely, since this was the only way to win the loyalty of 'each side's' respective Germans.

THE SEPARATE DEVELOPMENT OF THE OCCUPATION ZONES: PRELUDE TO DIVISION, 1945–1949

General conditions

In 1945, the circumstances in which the Germans found themselves in their different occupation zones, particularly their economic circumstances, were initially more or less the same. The main factors governing their separate development were external ones, especially the occupying powers, whose different systems determined their different policies towards Germany. On the whole, the policies put into effect in the zones of the three western, democratic occupying powers were milder than those in the zone controlled by the Stalinist USSR. In the absence of a Peace Treaty, the victorious powers at first adhered to the Potsdam Agreement as a general guideline: denazification, the elimination of Prussian militarism, dismantlement and reparations, the treatment of Germany west of the Oder-Neiße line as a single political unit divided into what were intended to be merely temporary occupation zones – this was the framework of the Allies' policy.

Intensification of the Cold War speeded up the process of dividing Germany. The stages were briefly as follows: the Marshall Plan of 1947 as the US answer to the communist civil war in Greece; the communist coup in Prague in February 1948; currency reform in the western zones and West Berlin in June 1948; the Soviet blockade of Berlin in 1948/49 and the airlift as the western powers' response; the Parliamentary Council in 'Trizonia' in 1948/49 and the People's Congress in the Soviet zone; the setting up of NATO in April 1949; the coming into effect of the Basic Law on 23 May 1949; the founding of the Federal Republic in August/September 1949 and of the GDR on 7 October 1949. Formally, the communist side was the more restrained at each stage, so that in sheer chronology the western side had the initiative. But as recently discovered documents show, Moscow had already decided in the spring of 1945 to split Germany if necessary by organizing their zone on soviet lines – that is, if they failed to take over the whole country.

Currency reform in the three western zones on 21 June 1948 was of more than symbolic importance. The new currency, the *Deutsche Mark*, provided access to the consumer society and to world markets for raw materials and industrial goods, but it split the Germans politically as well: 'real money' was the issue at the beginning of the division of Germany in 1948 just as it was when that division was overcome in 1990.

The Soviet occupation zone

Victory over the Third Reich presented Stalin with an opportunity finally to extend the communist revolution to Germany – an opportunity which had been missed in 1919/20, 1923 and 1933. Consequently, the Stalinist USSR carried out the 'antifascist transformation' of their occupation zone into a communist outpost with the utmost rigour, moderated only for propaganda reasons, in order to win German cooperation. Economically, the Soviets exploited their zone, with massive demands for reparation and dismantlement with which to reconstruct the western areas of their own country, destroyed in the war by the Germans. Even more devastating in the long term was the imposition of a centrally planned command economy. Nationalization and forced collectivization of industry and agriculture facilitated the growth of heavy industry, along soviet lines, which was obsessed with output – mainly arms production – using up men, machines and natural resources in huge quantities.

The 'socialist reorganization' of agriculture and industry, inaugurated by expropriation and the elimination of the big agricultural landowners, originally enjoyed a degree of popular approval in post-war Germany, as can be seen from the fact that in a plebiscite held at the end of 1946 on a change to the constitution of Hesse, a proposal was approved that land-holdings over 100 hectares should be split up and redistributed.

Agrarian reform in the Soviet zone meant that hundreds of thousands of settlers did indeed receive land of their own as smallholders, though after 1952 and the forced collectivization in agricultural cooperatives, this land was taken away from them.

Economically, the Soviet zone suffered from the massive dismantling of industrial plant. The western powers prohibited further deliveries to the East from their zones, in particular from the Ruhr, after the Cold War got under way in 1947, so the USSR fell back on its own zone, extracting much more from it than it was entitled to by way of reparation.

Politically, the East German communists gained the upper hand with the help of the Soviet occupying power, though they initially tried to disguise their predominance, forcing a merger in 1946 with the eastern SPD to form the SED, with spurious parity in the joint leadership bodies between communist KPD and socialist SPD. From the end of 1947, the main instrument of the SED was the 'German People's Congress for Unity and Peace with Justice', a non-elected proto-parliament which gave an indication of how the GDR itself would be constituted – both formally and in propagandist terms, in perpetual protest against any moves to found a West German state.

In the long term, terror, forced indoctrination and regimentation alienated those affected by the imposed Soviet model. The Stalinist terror of the occupying power in collaboration with the German communists took a toll of some 60,000 lives. Arbitrary arrest of alleged 'war criminals' for 'anti-Soviet activities' or 'sabotage' occurred on a massive scale. Both the Soviet occupying power and, at first, the newly founded GDR as well, took over erstwhile Nazi concentration camps in which even social democratic members of the German Resistance now ended up, in some extreme cases only weeks after their 'liberation' by the Red Army.[1] One finds oneself staring into a sinister abyss leading directly from one totalitarian system to the next. The absence of free elections meant that opposition was not so much political and collective as predominantly individual: people 'voted with their feet'. Between the end of the war and the founding of the GDR in 1949, some two million people left the Soviet occupation zone, and between then and the building of the Berlin Wall in 1961, a further two million.

The three western occupation zones

In spite of all the initial hardships at the end of the war and the period immediately following, the USA, Britain and France nevertheless established a basis for western-style parliamentary democracy in their occupation zones. All in all, they treated 'their' Germans more civilly, albeit with characteristic nuances. Initially, the Americans were the more rigorous in enforcing their moral 'non-fraternization' with the Germans and in their concept of collective punishment through de-industrialization and 're-education'. On the other hand, in the harsh winter of 1946/47 the USA was the first to switch to aid for the German population going hungry, collectively through grain shipments and individually through CARE parcels.

As after the First World War, the initial dismantling of industrial plant in the West had the dialectical effect of stimulating industrial modernization: the most up-to-date industrial equipment replaced that which had been dismantled, while France and Britain in particular were left with plant which had stood them in good stead, but which was now becoming obsolete. Consequently, though this was certainly not the intention of the occupying powers, dismantlement gave additional impetus to the modernization of the West German economy, giving it a flying start over her western competitors, while the Soviets were often unable to turn the dismantled equipment to good use.

At the beginning of the Cold War the USA put its political relations with the western zones on a new pragmatic basis signalled by Secretary of State James Byrnes's Stuttgart speech of 6 September 1946. The West Germans responded no less pragmatically, without excessive ideological enthusiasm. First they had to adapt to western ways and become gradually acquainted with parliamentary democracy – something to which they merely paid lip service in the beginning, without fully absorbing it.

Parallel to this, West Germany was becoming socio-economically a part of the West. The gradual reconstruction of parliamentary democracy from the bottom up was matched by radical reforms to liberalize the economy: there were moves aimed at breaking up large combines, the removal of obstacles to a free market economy, replacing what remained of the guild system with freedom of trade. 'Bizonia' came into being on 1 January 1947 when the US zone merged with the British zone, and 'Trizonia' with the addition of the French zone on 8 April 1949. Inclusion in the Marshall Plan in 1948 created access both to credit and raw materials, and to the world market. Currency reform and Ludwig Erhard's policy of liberalizing the economy to the greatest possible extent released enormous further potential for growth. Added to this was the desire for renewed consumption after ten years of forced austerity, and the will to leave behind as quickly as possible the destruction and deprivations of the immediate post-war period and return to peacetime normality.

The costs of the occupation incurred by West Germany were considerable, but were less than what their own armed forces would have cost. By the time of the currency reform in mid-1948, the worst war damage to the infrastructure had been repaired. Loans, raw materials, export markets and an iron will in respect of both savings and consumption, laid the foundations for the West German 'Economic Miracle'. But it was only during the Korean War (1950–53) and thanks to the 'Korea boom' in the world economy that this really took off, while the USA, Britain and France – Germany's strongest competitors in the West – were increasingly burdened by the costs of rearming for their own wars, including American involvement in Korea and French involvement in Indochina.

Britain and France's status as victors and major powers was now largely a formality; the decisive factor in West Germany's continued development was the USA, the new world power. Systematic 're-education' and denazification were the start of a far-reaching reorientation process which left a lasting impression on at least part of the rising generation, as Germany emerged from the isolation of the Nazi regime, opened up to the world, subjected its own history to self-critical scrutiny, and turned towards democracy. The habits of active democracy were gradually acquired through free elections and experience in the rule of parliament – also at federal level from 1949. West German politicians essentially tried to take up where the Weimar Republic had left off, though this was denounced by the Left as a form of 'Restoration'.

Political reconstruction began – as was formally the case in the Soviet zone, too – from the bottom up, with the formation of new *Länder*, or federal states, and the first elections at local level. It was a great surprise to all concerned when the newly formed CDU/CSU – an alliance of predominantly conservative forces of the Catholic Centre Party and of Protestantism – emerged from the first elections after the War as the strongest party. The *Unionsparteien*, together constituting a new people's party, enabled Konrad Adenauer to become the leading political personality in post-war West Germany.

The new US policy after September 1946 was to win over the West Germans as allies against the communist East. But in the process of enlisting German scientists and other expert professionals, the Americans more often had recourse to those who had served the Third Reich, than to emigrants or members of the German Resistance. This had pernicious consequences for German domestic politics, for the outwardly smooth formal integration of the Federal Republic with the West was offset by a lasting disgruntlement among many of the rising generation of intellectuals.

TWO GERMAN STATES: FEDERAL REPUBLIC AND GERMAN DEMOCRATIC REPUBLIC, 1949–1989/90

For forty years, the two parts of Germany lived side by side, or to be more exact, drifted apart: from 1949 as the Federal Republic of Germany and the German Democratic Republic, but at first still under the full sovereignty of the occupying powers. Their constitutional structures also developed along separate paths, the Federal Republic renewing federal traditions, the GDR conforming to the centralist structure of its occupying power. It was only rearmament in the course of the Cold War which bestowed sovereignty on both states (more so in the case of the Federal Republic). The Federal Republic became part of the West, rising within ten years to become an economic power – now Europe's strongest. From 1957, its economic integration within the EEC, subsequently EC, was a far-ranging success, as was its political and military integration through entry into NATO. The GDR was similarly integrated into the Council for Mutual Economic Aid (COMECON) and the Warsaw Pact. The Federal Republic became a democratic, liberal, constitutional state under the rule of law, with at first a somewhat western-conservative complexion; the GDR, a Stalinist, subsequently post-Stalinist state, centrally controlled and based on left-wing totalitarianism. What began as grim confrontation in the Cold War was transformed after 1969 by social-liberal *Ostpolitik* into peaceful coexistence and the mutual recognition of two states, each with a 'different social order'.

The Federal Republic

The Federal Republic of Germany grew out of 'Trizonia' in 1949.[2] It had a Basic Law rather than a constitution, in order to underline its provisional nature and with the future unification of Germany in mind. But the overriding German experience was initially one of material, economic and political reconstruction, leading to the 'Economic Miracle'. Soon a new type of German became apparent – *homo oeconomicus*, a pure-bred member of the affluent society, concerned only with achieving and maintaining prosperity, basically non-political, but if political at all, then to the Right. The suppression of the Nazi past through hard work, economic success and good democratic behaviour, both at home and abroad, were the trademarks of fourteen years of CDU/CSU rule under Adenauer's chancellorship.

The opposing SPD, up to 1952 under Kurt Schumacher, sharply dissociated itself from communism, advocating instead a social-democratic planned economy combined with an emphasis on nationalism – as late as 1965 one slogan ran: 'Germany divided in three? Never!' But in spite of such attempts at overlooking the Nazi past as much as possible, critical intellectuals under the watchful eye of public opinion abroad nevertheless managed to bring about a comprehensive reappraisal of the Nazi past – one which went further than in previous comparable instances – through contemporary historiography, political education and in the courts.

The Korean War of 1950–53 marked the end of the first stage, though its effect was ambivalent. Economically, the 'Korea boom' speeded up recovery, initiating the German 'Economic Miracle'. Politically, it divided the Federal Republic through Adenauer's demand that it be allowed to rearm and become a full partner of the West in order to win sovereignty,[3] but at the initial cost of deepening the split in Germany. What can best be described as Adenauer's 'magnet theory' (in Schumacher's formulation – the first to describe it with such precision) was the strengthening of an economically attractive and politically stable Federal Republic, so that one day, 'reunification in peace and freedom' would become possible with the accession of the GDR. Underlying this was the premise that the Federal Republic should be clearly and firmly anchored in the West.

A long-term conception such as this demanded patience and strong nerves, for it was gambling on the eventual peaceful collapse of communism and the USSR. Adenauer's conception later led to people becoming accustomed to the division of Germany, for in power-strategic terms, two German states offered a welcome opportunity to neutralize what would again have been a disproportionate German potential by turning it to the good of Europe and a new balance of power.

Adenauer's conception has been borne out by events, though not without some detrimental effects: his unembarrassed, conservative recourse to broad swathes of the administrative élites of the Third Reich alienated very many young intellectuals from him personally, and from the Federal Republic. So, too, did his relative failure to convince sceptics of the wisdom of his policy of anchoring the Federal Republic in the West. In the event, the unification of Germany came about only through the *Ostpolitik* of the social-liberal coalition of Brandt and Scheel, a policy which Adenauer's CDU/CSU party, in opposition after 1969, initially rejected, then itself implemented in tacit agreement after returning to power in 1982. But conversely, it is also true that, had the Federal Republic not been anchored in the West, the opening up to the East would, in world-political terms, have been by no means certain; while without the opening up to the East, the anchoring of the Federal Republic in the West would have left it immured in the sterile political cul-de-sac of the Cold War.

In retrospect, the Federal Republic's first major crisis seems almost to have been predetermined: people had grown weary of the 'Grand Old Man' Adenauer and the stagnation he had come to embody. The mellowing of the communist system after Stalin's death was reflected abroad in the phase of 'peaceful coexistence' and *détente*, during which the Federal Republic was in danger of becoming isolated even in the West. In addition, there was criticism of the authoritarian way in which dissent at home was handled (the *Spiegel* affair of 1962), greater awareness of Third World conflicts (the Algerian and Vietnam wars, the decolonization of Africa), the repercussions of the first economic recession after 1966, the fall of Erhard's hapless government and the entry of the nationalist NPD into most state parliaments in the Federal Republic: all this and many other factors merged in a simmering malaise.

As a new political generation grew up, their criticisms and feelings of resentment combined with the disillusionment which commonly sets in when a ruling party has enjoyed a long period of unchallenged supremacy, to produce an explosive mixture: the sons and daughters of *homo oeconomicus* rebelled in a typical generation conflict. Having grown up in affluence and freedom in a constitutional state under the rule of law – the first time that such things had been taken for granted – the new *homo ideologicus* of the Left denounced the West's shortcomings and inadequate prosecution of its Nazi past, with a rigour that was ultimately self-defeating, rendering him blind to the much greater failings of communism.

The Grand Coalition of 1966–69 between CDU/CSU and SPD under Kiesinger and Brandt became itself an expression of this malaise. Its effect was mixed. On the one hand it was able, in purely technocratic terms, to overcome the 1966 recession, and it also took the first cautious steps towards the East. On the other, as a maxi-coalition with its emergency powers legislation and its opportunistic silence over US involvement in the Vietnam War (which had been escalating since February 1965), it provoked protest against the new status quo, especially among the up-and-coming intelligentsia. The 'extra-parliamentary opposition' of the 1968 student movement produced the Federal Republic's first domestic crisis – comparable with similar events elsewhere, especially in France, Italy and the USA.

After two decades of conservative renaissance under the CDU/CSU, the backlog of pressure for modernization found a political outlet. The '68 movement and the social-liberal coalition of Brandt and Scheel from 1969 vigorously shook up the rigidity of West German society, again with mixed results: as it had opened up to the West, so now, at least intellectually, it opened up to the East. Among many of the intelligentsia, especially the young, there was a neo-Marxist renaissance with idealistic, romanticizing overtones. *Homo ideologicus*'s leanings were to the Left. His clash with the older *homo oeconomicus* triggered off a drive to modernize the political process, but also a serious crisis which troubled the hitherto mainly economic and formal political links with the West: neo-Marxism cultivated an uncritical and idealized image of ruling communism.

But on the whole, the crisis was a productive one. The Federal Republic experienced for the first time something fundamental to all western democracies – permanent evolution and reform, as distinct from the outbreaks of violence and sporadic use of force in authoritarian, and even more in totalitarian, systems. Practice in the workings of pluralism and social flexibility were perhaps the greatest gains from the '68 movement. As for the New Left, the internal liberalization of the Federal Republic was at least potentially endangered by a new dogmatism that could even be seen as the West German version of a Cultural Revolution.

There was a convergence of several factors. The social-liberal government's general amnesty regarding all pending legal proceedings arising out of the student movement (but not including the arsonists responsible for burning down a Frankfurt department store as a gesture against the Vietnam War) split the '68 movement. One wing proclaimed a 'march through the institutions' (Rudi Dutschke) and fanned out into a whole spectrum of the Left. Part of the 'extra-parliamentary opposition' joined the newly founded communist DKP, a merger of older cadres from the KPD which had been banned in 1956 and young activists from the intelligentsia. In addition, there were Maoist groupings taking their cue from China's Cultural Revolution – as romanticized from a distance. Many of them later formed a core of the Greens and the 'Alternatives', while others withdrew from politics into sheer hedonism. Those of the New Left who were pragmatists joined the SPD straight away. Conversely, those who had been omitted from the general amnesty worked themselves up into 'revolutionary' activism, culminating in the terror of the Red Army Faction, the 'Movement of the second of June' and the 'Red Cells', directed against the liberal constitutional state under the rule of law.

Some of the '68 generation carried Marxist dogma over into their various careers. The relatively positive view they retained of communism and 'real existing socialism', including that of the GDR, developed into a rigorous 'antifascist' anti-anticommunism which condemned all criticism of communism as 'anticommunist'. At the same time, an aversion to the idea of a German nation spread. Most on the Left, for different motives, were hostile to any reunification of the nation-state. Rejection based on a sense of responsibility towards Europe – as long as the USSR was still intact as a world power and stood in the way of peaceful reunification – was entirely rational, ultimately leading to the idea of a German confederation if only the GDR could democratize itself internally. On the other hand, the argument that the Germans should not be allowed to found a nation-state again as punishment for Auschwitz (Günter Grass) was a moralizing one. Many on the Left in West Germany harboured the dogmatic hope that the GDR could keep going as an experimental laboratory, though without themselves being willing to go there and take an active part in the construction of real existing socialism.

After the liberating success of its new *Ostpolitik*, SPD politics gradually drifted into immobility. From the middle of the 1970s, it abandoned its ideological confrontation with communist regimes and elevated antifascist anti-anticommunism almost to the level of party doctrine. In the end, it made a self-justifying fetish of good relations with the USSR and the GDR, even after the Soviet war in Afghanistan in 1979 and the chronic crisis in Poland since 1980/81.[4] The new left wing of the party withdrew its support from Helmut Schmidt in the autumn of 1982, precipitating his fall by means of a 'constructive vote of no confidence' in the *Bundestag*.

In opposition after October 1982, the SPD's stance in practice became increasingly one of appeasement towards ruling communism. One example of this was the campaign of 1982/83 against deployment of cruise missiles by the Americans, in which half of the leadership were clearly members of the DKP, political control of the campaign consequently being in the hands of the SED. At least some members of the SPD participated in a semi-official capacity, as they did later in the *Historikerstreit* of 1986, resisting what they interpreted as attempts to relativize the crimes of Nazism by some West German historians.[5] Another instance was the joint SPD-SED paper of 1987, at a time when the SPD was carefully avoiding contact with the opposition in what were still the communist Eastern bloc countries.[6] Even in the last days of the social-liberal coalition, Nobel prize winner Willy Brandt openly attacked the Polish Solidarity Movement, before the eyes of all the world, and the SPD Chancellor Helmut Schmidt agreed with the First Secretary of the SED, Erich Honecker, on 13 December 1981 in welcoming martial law in Poland. In opposition to Helmut Kohl after 1982, the SPD abandoned its fundamental positions *vis-à-vis* the GDR (including common German citizenship) and consulted behind the scenes with the SED leadership on how to conduct its own election campaigns, in exchange for spectacular concessions from the GDR in return. In general, one can say that the Left, including the SPD, through its one-sided ideological bias rendered itself remarkably blind to the imminent collapse of Soviet communism, as heralded by the war in Afghanistan and the chronic turmoil in Poland.

All in all, whatever ritual noises the government might make about 'German unity', the Federal Republic had ultimately come to terms with the division of Germany. It concentrated on humanitarian easings in a divided Germany; even the evident agony of the USSR under Gorbachev from 1985 onwards did nothing to change this stance.

The German Democratic Republic

The founding of the GDR was intended to set up a political framework for the eventual political and/or military victory of 'real socialism' in Germany as a whole. But in the long term, the GDR remained shackled to the fundamental weaknesses of the Soviet Union and the communist 'world system', incapable of surmounting these obstacles by its own efforts. Even the best intentions of many GDR citizens and their genuine personal commitment to 'the construction of socialism' could not prevail in these circumstances. Politically, the GDR was more of a counter-productive deterrent to communism as it was actually practised. Nevertheless, skilful communist propaganda was able to cultivate illusions among a section of the Left in the West in general, and the Federal Republic in particular, as to the true character of communism, especially after 1968 – a year of symbolic significance.

The 'first workers' and peasants' state' always portrayed itself as the 'better Germany', the one that had 'learned the right lessons' from history. But a stream of new revelations since unification confirms that just about everything that antifascist left-wingers in the West had denounced as malicious anticommunist propaganda, refusing to believe it, was in fact quite close to the truth, or indeed was often surpassed by the now visible reality of 'real socialism'. No wonder that the historical assessment of the GDR has become more sombre since 1989/90.

There was a harsh break in 1945 from right-wing Nazi dictatorship to forty-five years of left-wing totalitarian rule in the Soviet occupation zone/GDR. It was imposed from without, but maintained internally with steely determination by German cadres under Wilhelm Pieck, Walter Ulbricht and Erich Honecker. Running counter to this break with the Nazi past and the antifascist pathos of communist propaganda, however, there were many examples of continuity – both of totalitarian methods (repression, monolithic one-party state, continued use of concentration camps) and the deployment of any Nazi personnel willing to submit to the new authority. The general militarization of the GDR – from the National People's Army and border guards, workers' militia branches and brigades of agricultural and industrial workers, right down to schools, pre-military training and the glorification of the country's army literally from kindergarten upwards – is one of the most depressing examples of the wrong sort of continuities taken over from the Third Reich.

Thus, from the outset, the 'humanistic' GDR shared the basically criminal character of totalitarian Soviet communism, though, it is true, at a lower level of violence than the Stalinist Soviet Union itself. The 'past which will not pass' finally and inexorably caught up with the GDR as well. This mortgage of guilt finally brought about its collapse, in conformity with the fundamental crisis of communism in power: every internal crisis in the Soviet sphere of influence, directly or indirectly, sooner or later, affected the GDR as well, it being the Soviet Empire's most exposed outpost in Europe.

No matter how moderate and reformist the GDR might have become, it could never escape from this dialectic both repressing it and generally forcing it into line with the Soviet system. This fateful connection should never be lost sight of: the slogan of a party which was supposedly always right – 'To learn from the Soviet Union is to learn victory' – was turned on its head as it faced defeat. It was precisely Honecker's desperate attempts to cut the tow rope and break away from Gorbachev's reform policies after 1985 which finished off the GDR: it was dragged under as Real Socialism sank. Yet again, Sallust's 2,000-year-old insight has proved correct: the same factors which make a state also break it.

Initially, the Soviet occupation zone/GDR appeared to carry on Germany's federal traditions, its five new *Länder* (federal states) on the ruins of the Third Reich a parallel to the reconstitution of federal states in the western zones. At the height of the Cold War, however, in 1952, the SED abolished the *Länder*, replacing them with 15 administrative regions (*Bezirke*) in a centralized unitary state rigorously controlled from top to bottom, in which self-government disappeared at even the most local level. Parallel to the forced nationalization and collectiviza-tion of industry and agriculture, the SED also eradicated what remained of the rule of law by bringing justice into line with the system, and abolished 'bourgeois' structures in schools and higher education. At the same time, the SED regime isolated itself and its people against West Germany with barbed wire, minefields and spring-gun installa-tions, largely sealing off the GDR from the West's innovations at the same time. All this was safeguarded by a state security apparatus which, in the extent and intensity of its repression, far surpassed the Gestapo in the Third Reich, even during the Second World War.

Yet the GDR leadership, in line with Moscow, went on the offensive over the German Question. Its thrust against the founding of the Fed-eral Republic and for the GDR's 'all-German peace policy' are in stark contrast to the offensive military plans for war which recent disclosures since unification have established – an atomic blitzkrieg against the Federal Republic to make possible a rapid advance to the Atlantic and the Pyrenees. In 1953 at least, more teachers than the country itself needed were trained, the justification being that they would teach in West German schools after the East had brought about reunification. The grotesque surplus of officers and generals in the National People's Army, even in 1990, can be similarly explained.

As a communist state based on coercion, the long-term structures of the GDR doomed it to ultimate failure, even though its mixed agrarian-industrial structure allowed it to enjoy the highest standard of living in the Soviet Empire. Every attempt to reduce these living standards to those of the Soviet Union and its heterogeneous peoples inevitably ran up against the resistance of the East Germans, especially since they were being simultaneously promised all the joys of socialism. As long as access to the West remained to some extent open, if necessary via Berlin after the closure of the border with West Germany in 1952, millions of East Germans could escape Stalinist coercion by 'illegal emigration' to the Federal Republic. But the more the GDR regime insulated itself, the less able it became to release externally the constant excess pressure of dissatisfaction.

Consequently, it was in the GDR, caught between the seeming stability of the monolithic Stalinist Soviet Union and the unpredictability of its European satellites, that the paradox between external delimitation and increased danger of internal implosion first became manifest. In the general uncertainty following the 'thaw' in the USSR after Stalin's death on 5 March 1953, the SED leadership itself provoked the protest of workers in the heavy industry that its own ideology had nurtured and pampered – the steelworkers of Hennigsdorf. A lowering of the standard of living caused by a raising of production norms led to a general strike on 16 June that year. On 17 June, social and economic demands rapidly turned into political demands – free elections, which would have led to the foreseeable overthrow of SED rule. The SED could only quell the revolt with the help of Soviet tanks and bloodshed.

For the GDR, 17 June 1953 was a lasting trauma. While many fled to the West, the silent majority of the population came to terms with the system and sought out a suitable niche – to a greater or lesser degree, a non-political one. But outward conformism was deceptive and concealed a growing alienation between the ruled and their rulers, who in any case – as Bertolt Brecht put it – could not dissolve the people and elect another. The government remained scared stiff of its own citizens, for whose good it was supposedly working, and greatly expanded the secret police (*Stasi*).

At the same time, the events of 17 June 1953 revealed for the first time outside the Soviet Union, where comparable events at local level could be more easily screened from world opinion, a fundamental flaw in all totalitarian systems and one which caused the destruction both of Soviet communism and its East German offshoot – their incapacity to undertake structural reform. Since all attempts at reform were in any case departures from a (frequently changing) party line, and consequently a capital offence, even reform aimed at preserving the system, or giving way on certain selective issues under pressure from below, was thought to be the beginning of the end of the 'revolutionary' system (in reality, a fossilized oligarchy). An inexorable domino effect ensured that crises endemic to the Soviet Empire were passed on to the GDR.

The next crisis in the Soviet system, sparked off by a second wave of de-Stalinization after Khruschchev's 'secret speech' at the Twentieth Party Congress of the Communist Party of the Soviet Union in February 1956, seemed to pass the GDR by without trace. But the uprisings in Poland and Hungary in the autumn of 1956, and their suppression, precipitated an internal struggle for power at the top of the system – a characteristic of such crises – between communist 'reformers' urging a pragmatic change of course, and those who were later known in Poland as the 'concrete skulls'.

The Federal Republic had joined NATO in 1955, and the USSR now used the enclave of West Berlin as a pawn in the continuing 'clash of the systems' to force the Federal Republic and her western allies to ratify the *de facto* division of German statehood in international law. In 1958, the threat to close Berlin, the last means of escape, accelerated the massive exodus of refugees and the bleeding white of the GDR from within. To stop this self-inflicted population haemorrhage, the SED made its most spectacular mistake so far: on 13 August 1961, it began to build the Berlin Wall. This finally sealed off the GDR from the West, at the expense of a global crisis which could have escalated into armed confrontation between the occupation powers in Berlin. New documents from Moscow show for the first time that SED First Secretary Walter Ulbricht wanted to eliminate the enclave of West Berlin by a military strike, even at the risk of a third world war. But as this is exactly what Khruschchev wanted to avoid, he turned the SED regime's desperate plan into a compromise between doing nothing and Ulbricht's projected all-out attack – he closed off Berlin, which in turn led to the Berlin Wall.[7] The SED made desperate attempts to pass the Wall off to the world as an 'antifascist protective wall', though its main function was obvious: to prevent any more GDR citizens from going west.

Even so, the effect was ambivalent. On the one hand, the Wall discredited the SED regime in the eyes of public opinion throughout much of the world, while yet giving the regime a chance to increase, or partially justify through more liberal measures, the relative domestic stability it had achieved by force. After some half-hearted attempts, however, the Ulbricht regime soon reverted to its former oppressive rigidity.

On the other hand, the Berlin Wall literally made concrete the division of Germany into two states. In the most directly affected part of the West, namely West Berlin under its Mayor Willy Brandt, the new realities prompted a rethink which led to the *Ostpolitik* of the social-liberal coalition beginning in the autumn of 1969: there can be no doubt that 'change through rapprochement' (Egon Bahr) was intended as change on *both* sides. After the Cuba crisis of 1962, it was the Soviet Union which conducted its new 'charm offensive' of world-wide *détente* and 'peaceful coexistence'. But its dynamic destroyed Soviet communism in less than thirty years by exposing its inability to reform for all the world to see. Treaties with the Eastern bloc countries in 1970–72 could not exclude the GDR from the new openings for travel, though the SED reacted with even more oppressive 'ideological delimitation'. It could, however, point to the international recognition of the GDR and its acceptance, along with the Federal Republic, into the United Nations, as positive gains in 1973.

As the next stage in *détente*, the Soviet Union pressed for the Conference on Security and Collaboration in Europe (CSCE), to which the West coupled the question of human rights. The communist East was already so weak economically that it was forced to swap the principle of human rights for economic links. From the time of the Helsinki Conference in 1975, the issue of human rights was like dynamite on a time fuse, since it was in the very nature of communism to disregard and flout human rights. Beginning with 'Charter 77' in Czechoslovakia and what were initially individual human rights groups even in the USSR, oppositional circles in the GDR also gradually began to invoke the spirit of Helsinki. But fundamentally, right up to the events of 1989, these groups did not want to abolish the GDR, but only, by way of reform, to bring about a better, truly democratic GDR.

Unification through the collapse of the GDR, 1979–1989

The history of German unification up to the fall of the Berlin Wall can best be understood as the self-dissolution of the GDR in the wake of communism's death throes. As the very viability of the USSR became critical since the beginning of the war in Afghanistan in late 1979, so the GDR too entered its final death-throes, which the chronic crisis in Poland in 1980/81 made inevitable. At home, the SED mobilized a considerable amount of traditional anti-Polish resentment towards the Solidarity movement; conversely, Solidarity became the secret hero of the eastern world on account of its oppositional stance. When martial law was declared in Poland on 13 December 1981, it probably came as a surprise to Honecker to find the social-democratic Chancellor of the Federal Republic, Helmut Schmidt, agreeing with him over the need to maintain stability in the Polish People's Republic.

On the issue of cruise missile deployment, Honecker took up a relatively independent and sensible position compared with Moscow, arguing for the 'common responsibility of the two Germanies', and against the nuclear missiles as 'diabolical devices'. To be sure, this did not curtail the GDR's influence over the West German Peace Movement, after the fall of the social-liberal coalition in October 1982, through the communist DKP and its fellow travellers, thereby increasing the ideological distance between itself and the West. More and more citizens of the GDR who would not conform, who expressed their dissent and invoked the CSCE resolution, or who even applied to emigrate (which they could now legally do), were deemed to have joined the 'enemy within'.

The standard of living declined *vis-à-vis* the West and the neighbouring Federal Republic, but also *vis-à-vis* the East and the other Eastern bloc countries. The GDR economy overstretched itself, at huge cost, through the central planning of the command economy, obfuscation of political and economic processes by means of secret or doctored statistics, lack of public supervision, obsolescence of industrial plant, sinking productivity, over-manning with actual underlying unemployment, high expenditure on armaments, parasitic multiple bureaucracies with their additional privileges, costly social services – all in order to keep its citizens happy. By 1983 the GDR was almost bankrupt; this was only temporarily avoided by loans amounting to two thousand million DM, arranged by the man GDR propaganda labelled communism's 'archenemy', Franz Josef Strauß. In reality, the collapse of the GDR was imminent. It is unlikely that Brezhnev, with his doctrine that any state that had once become communist would necessarily remain so forever, would have peacefully accepted the developments of 1989/90.

The turning point was brought about only by Gorbachev's policy of reform, which was really intended to save the system. The refusal of the GDR's leadership to go along with these reforms sealed East Germany's fate. After the banning of the Soviet magazine *Sputnik*, most GDR citizens, who wanted *perestroika* in their own country, pinned their hopes on 'Gorby'. Honecker's state visit to the Federal Republic and the joint SPD-SED paper of 1987 were merely illusory triumphs for the GDR on its path to proper recognition in the world. In fact, Honecker put the screws on again at home immediately afterwards. Apart from Ceauçescu's Romania, the GDR regime was the only state which supported the Tienanmen Square massacre of June 1989, obliquely threatening a similar reaction should a comparable situation occur.

With the installation of the Mazowiecki government in Poland in September 1989, a GDR incapable of reform found itself isolated between the reforming East (Poland, USSR) and the democratic West. After Hungary opened its border to Austria and refugees began to flood into the West, first through Hungary but then also via the West German embassies in Prague and Warsaw, the GDR was past saving. Only open repression, the 'Chinese solution', could deal with the rapidly swelling demonstrations. Every historical precedent indicates that such repression would certainly have caused the collapse of the regime, but this time with an accompanying bloodbath. The nightmare scenario of Tienanmen Square provided all sides with an incentive to keep the democratic revolution a peaceful one: 'No violence!' was one of the demonstrators' slogans, and at the last moment those responsible in the regime shied away from causing a bloodbath.

The gulf between the pompous official celebrations on the fortieth anniversary of the GDR, and reality, finished Honecker off politically. Gorbachev, discreetly enjoying the crowd in East Berlin during an official state visit, confronted the Politburo of the SED with a truth for home consumption: 'who comes late is punished by life'. With his blunt assertion that no one would 'shed a single tear' for those emigrating illegally, Honecker dug his own grave and that of the GDR. Under pressure from the continuing peaceful Monday demonstrations, especially those in Leipzig, Honecker's removal on 18 October 1989 and the opening of the Wall on 9 November merely reflected last-minute panic, which nevertheless opened the way to unity.

The changing slogans of the Monday demonstrations in Leipzig show how the otherwise unpublished opinion of the GDR population changed: 'We stay here!' and 'We are the people!' were still internal, directed solely against the SED which professed to represent the people and to be active on its behalf. 'Gorby, help us!' was an appeal for help to the leader of what had hitherto been the dominant power, and against the SED regime. 'We are one people!' took up once again the all-German dimension of 17 June 1953 and extended it, but this time no Soviet tanks moved in to prop up the SED regime.

It was Egon Krenz – trusted by nobody after he had approved the Tienanmen Square massacre – who unwittingly provided the term subsequently applied to the collapse of the GDR – *Wende*, or 'turning point' – though by it he meant the salvation of the GDR. But after the opening of the Berlin Wall, under growing internal pressure, the GDR was doomed.

The first transitional government under Hans Modrow (SED) bowed to the move towards inevitable unity, but tried to erase the worst traces of SED rule from the records, and to instigate a 'march through the institutions' by SED cadres. After the first free election to the East German Parliament on 18 March 1990, the second transitional government of Lothar de Maizière (CDU) merely presided over the winding up of the GDR, which was completed by 3 October 1990.

5 United Germany since 1989/90

Through unification, the Germans found a new answer – this time a seemingly conclusive one – to the chronic German Question. Once again, they have their own nation-state, with clearly defined borders, extending to the Oder-Neiße line in the east. Thanks to Gorbachev, unification was a peaceful process – rare enough, for such a tremendous shift in the balance of power. Germany's traditional federal structure was retained internally, and externally extended by its integration within an increasingly integrated Europe (EC, CSCE, NATO, Council of Europe). That leaves internal unity still to be achieved, and the need to find a place in Europe for an enlarged and (at least on paper) more powerful Germany, without once again tearing the continent apart.

But it would run counter to every historical precedent if the consequences of unification were as smooth and unproblematical as unification itself. The German Question will remain, though it will confront the Germans in a different form. How will they adapt to each other and cope with the far-reaching consequences of unification? How will they use their new power, at home and abroad? Internal and external problems lead inexorably to balancing acts riven by tension and conflict, incompatible with any cheap sense of triumph. Straddling East and West, the newly united Germans now find themselves torn in every possible direction. For an onlooker who is also directly involved and affected, it is difficult to maintain the necessary inner distance and objectivity and to refrain from writing satirically about the sense of confusion in the unified Germany: for forty years the Germans bewailed their division; since unification they bemoan the fact that they now have to share.

FROM NEW UNITY TO INTERNAL DIVISION

Once they were roused, it was the citizens of the GDR who provided the real momentum for unity, both before and after the collapse of the Wall. The Federal Republic simply watched in amazement; hardly anyone there still wanted unification, apart from pious national faith-healers. The political classes of the Federal Republic had had no accurate foresight of the crisis which enveloped the whole of the communist East. They were consequently unprepared for unity, and the problems to which it gave rise: there were no plans; suddenly unity was upon them. The result was total confusion.

9 November 1989: 'mad euphoria' and 'Trabi fever'; dissolution of the GDR, 1989/90

For a few weeks after the Wall fell, 'mad euphoria' – *Wahnsinn* – and the exhilaration of the 'Trabi exodus' reached fever pitch, appearing at first to drown all sensible reflection in the general intoxication. 'The happiest people on earth' (Momper) should 'let what belongs together grow together' (Brandt), but were not sure how. It was already clear on the evening of 9 November 1989 that the real problems were just about to begin, as the westward exodus swelled. Westerners speculated against the weak East German Mark, unscrupulously buying up subsidized food from under the noses of GDR citizens, with East German Marks they had exchanged at ridiculously low rates, and occupying restaurants with their similarly subsidized low prices. West Berlin firms posted their correspondence in East Berlin to take advantage of the lower postal charges there. Conversely, East Germans went west and offered their services at moonlight rates. Even the *Bundesbahn*, normally the epitome of punctuality, suddenly had hour-long delays on its inter-city trains after 10 November. Chaos within Germany was imminent. A quick solution was absolutely essential.

Helmut Kohl, who up to then had been a rather hapless, lacklustre chancellor, seized with both hands the opportunity to enter the history books as a second Bismarck, as Adenauer's political heir in bringing about unification 'in peace and liberty'. Faced with insistent pressure from the East German population, only one solution was politically acceptable: access as soon as possible to the DM, the only 'real' money people recognized, apart from the dollar. The final slogan of the now literally mobile East Germans on the path to unity was an ominous warning: 'If the D-Mark does not come to us, we will go to the D-Mark!'

Exhibiting a robust instinct for power, Kohl swiftly took all the right foreign policy steps, with the exception of his embarrassingly long hesitation before recognizing the Oder-Neiße line. He coolly turned a blind eye to other risks, such as the economic risks. Of course, it would have been theoretically more sensible to have tackled unification more slowly – for instance, by means of a confederation, to draw the whole process out over a period of twenty to thirty years. But that was not how things stood, for the East Germans' fear of being overtaken by more repressive events ruled out any alternative schemes, which became merely academic speculation. So – for political reasons – there was no alternative to the sequence of events adopted by Kohl: first currency and social union, then political union. It was also sensible to integrate the newly united Germany irrevocably within Europe, in order to prevent any repetition of German hegemonic tendencies.

Thus, in the first free elections to the People's Chamber of Deputies on 18 March 1990, the Eastern CDU won a surprisingly clear victory on traditional SPD territory. The next provisional government under Lothar de Maizière merely implemented the voluntary self-dissolution of the GDR through its rapid accession to the Federal Republic on 3 October 1990. As on New Year's Eve 1989 at the Brandenburg Gate, the Germans were once again (still) able to celebrate their political unification with glittering parties.[1]

In the summer of 1990, Kohl coolly exploited the final agony of the USSR, which – as had been the case following Russia's withdrawal from the continent after the Crimean War – now opened the way to German unification, but which also uncoupled the citizens of the GDR from the impending chaos. Talks in the Caucasus with Gorbachev gave Germany a chance to unite peacefully by securing the consent of the USSR, necessary in international law, with strategic and financial concessions in the Two-plus-Four Treaty. Kohl gave the Soviets a golden opportunity to make an honourable retreat from positions which had become morally and politically untenable. In retrospect, the collapse of the Soviet Union since the attempted coup of August 1991 amply justifies Kohl's resolute initiative. What might have happened if the putsch had been successful, and the Soviet Army, National People's Army and *Stasi* had still had full power and authority to act in a still existent GDR, doesn't bear thinking about.

The newly dividing nation, post–1990

Against the 'Chancellor of Unity' and his apparent all-round success, the SPD stood no chance in the first all-German elections to the

Bundestag in December 1990, especially as the image it projected could not have been weaker. Lacking any self-criticism, after a decade of what had amounted to appeasement towards ruling communism, it became obsessed with various kinds of populism: a newly awakened national populism was cultivated by honorary chairman Willy Brandt, and social populism by Oskar Lafontaine, the nominee for the chancellorship. Lafontaine repeatedly stressed (in realistic estimates) the cost involved in unification, but gave the impression that the SPD wanted to shirk unification because its financial burden would be too great.

Consequently, domestic confusion after unification hit the SPD first and hardest, before inexorably spreading to the whole country. To this one can add what appears to be a structural incapacity for dealing openly and clearly, through lucid analysis, with the secularized, messianic-apocalyptic wing of early social democracy, which had gone independent as KPD and SED, but which after 1968 filtered back into the SPD. In spite of all its regional successes in *Landtag* elections, the SPD seems to have established its incompetence to rule at national or federal level for the foreseeable future.

On the other hand, almost everything Kohl did domestically went wrong. Very soon after the federal election, he was made aware of the price to be paid for the short-sighted populism which had led him to take the propagandist path of least resistance, promising that unification would be an easy stroll for all concerned. Instead of coming clean to the Germans in both East and West about the cost of unification, he had lulled them into a false sense of security, giving the West Germans the impression that paying for unification (and beyond that, meeting the escalating costs of the post-communist plight in eastern and south-eastern Europe) would be peanuts, without increased taxes or additional public borrowing, while promising the East Germans that no one would be worse off than before. But in the second all-German federal election at the end of 1994, the 'tax lie' (Lafontaine) in the West and the 'affluence lie' in the East were not enough to bring to an end Kohl's all-German chancellorship, because no viable alternative was in sight.

A more realistic estimate of the cost of unification could have been possible at the outset, on 9 November 1989: the West Germans, who had basked on the sunny side of the German divide for forty years, should have been asked to pay up to demonstrate true solidarity with their 'brothers and sisters in the East'. In response, the East Germans should have been obliged to show patience and understanding for the initial transitional hardships unavoidably caused by the break-up of their *ancien régime*, until such time as a new order had been established.

Economic parity with the West will take at least a decade, since too rapid an increase in purchasing power without a corresponding rise of productivity in the East would inevitably plunge the now all-German DM into an inflationary spiral.

East–West confusion and confrontations

Unity plunged the Germans into the grip of an all-German hangover which put a stop to any further jubilation over unification. Unhappily reunited, if they carry on this way there is every chance they could split up again, though this time – unlike after 1945 – without foreign intervention. The confusion in the new Germany is understandable: initial chaos after the collapse of a system is normal. Only gradually did the full extent of the GDR's total bankruptcy become clear – agriculture and industry, infrastructure and decaying cities, the self-inflicted contamination of natural resources – both material (ecological over-exploitation) and psychological (*Stasi*, censorship, repression). No society can endure forty-five years of left-wing totalitarian dictatorship following on from twelve years of right-wing totalitarian dictatorship without bearing deep wounds. In spite of visits to and from relatives and access to West German television in the GDR, the two parts of Germany were more alienated from each other than anyone had suspected. In macro-economic terms, the GDR is certainly no cheap 'asset' (Günter Grass), even if many individual West Germans reaped the fruits of unification. On the contrary, for the foreseeable future it is an indigestible mouthful of nasty tastes from the past which will continue to lie heavily on West German stomachs.

The decisive factor is the economic gap between West and East, and its social, political and psychological consequences. Only after unification did it emerge that per capita economic power and productivity in the East was only about a third of the corresponding levels in the West: all of a sudden, the 'dear brothers and sisters' in the East turned into tiresome poor relations from the outback.

East Germans, liberated from communism, feel as if they have been recolonized, and that is indeed how many West Germans have been behaving: streaming eastward like sharks to take profitable bites from the living flesh. Especially at first, unsuspecting *Ossis* were easily taken for a ride by large-scale swindlers and small-time con-men from the West operating under the guise of the new liberty. Whole industrial plants were sold for one symbolic Deutschmark – a favourite trick, condoned by the *Treuhand* government agency, which appeared to turn a blind eye as would-be investors (West German or foreign) stripped the factories of most of their assets, driving them into bankruptcy and the workers concerned into unemployment, instead of modernizing them. Another method for at least one big (West German) concern was to pretend to take over a potential rival, siphon off know-how and the brightest brains and then snatch away orders on the reconstruction market in East Germany. Sometimes there was a combination of both procedures.

This was outright white-collar criminality under the cloak of establishing the 'free market society', confirming the worst propaganda slogans of the former SED, and of course causing bad blood with the millions of victims left behind in an industrial wasteland where Helmut Kohl had promised 'flourishing provinces' in spring 1990. Many were, indeed, much worse off than before, although the Chancellor had promised before the March 1990 elections that 'none will be worse off'.

The principle of 'restitution before compensation', forced through by the West against strong opposition, has pulled the ground from beneath the feet of (literally) millions, while already well-to-do or rich West Germans lay claim to real estate and property in the East. After the iron hand was removed, and with it also 'collective anti-social criminality' under the surveillance of real existing socialism's police-state, individual criminality rose in the East, evidently as part of the price of 'normalization' with western liberty. Those bringing genuine aid, by contrast, whether official or individual, found it much more difficult to be accepted in the face of growing embitterment.

The widespread arrogance of swaggering West Germans who think they know better is matched by the often hypersensitive reactions of many *Ossis*. Losing their (albeit precarious) GDR identity – once unloved in both East and West, though for different reasons – had already made them amply unsure of themselves. All too often, individual *Wessis*, and the new order as a whole, now finish off what little remains of their self-confidence. If possible, everything from that era should simply disappear, even the (admittedly few) sensible things there also were, naturally enough: a zero alcohol limit when driving, and certain social and cultural institutions, particularly for the young.

While many West Germans act as if they blame the East Germans for having held out so long, or even for just living in the GDR in the first place, many East Germans in return give the impression of believing that West Germans, who have known only the security of the West, have no right even to talk about the GDR. Touchy to everything that looks like western criticism of the erstwhile GDR and its totalitarian character, too many take it personally, when such views are really only directed at collective political structures.

Although the unification process has caused hardships, with East

Germans suffering most at the beginning, it is easy to lose sight of the gains: liberty and the rule of law. If the *Wende* had gone in the opposite direction, after a victory of the SED/*Stasi* regime, it would have been a much less civil process. The main problems can be attributed to forty-five years of communist mismanagement. It is normal for mistakes to occur – some avoidable, some unavoidable – while the mess is sorted out. Had the GDR managed to protract its existence yet further, it could have drifted into open bankruptcy and the sort of post-communist chaos of Bosnia and elsewhere.

Financial, structural and personal aid from the former Federal Republic is at a level that countries such as Poland or Hungary can only dream of, but it also gnaws away at the *Ossis'* self-confidence. In absolute and relative terms, they are better off than their erstwhile socialist 'brother nations', but these, in turn, do not know the dilemma of being condescendingly embraced and all but crushed by one's own real, rich 'big brother'. All these factors have to be taken into account if one is to understand the emergence of a self-destructive nostalgia for the GDR, which the SED's successor, the PDS, openly embraces as part of its distinctive appeal.

Of course, any transition from a central command economy to a social market economy has its problems. Even Ludwig Erhard in 1948 did not effect the change overnight, but took it in relatively slow stages. Equally, there could have been more generous social measures in support of the joint 'Eastern Revival' (*Aufschwung Ost*) campaign, to give the eastern economy a kick-start. At the very least, experts should have been able to foresee and take into account the loss of former GDR markets in the ex-communist East, once the DM was introduced. Instead of privatization and the reduction of an inflated workforce through radical 'rationalization', it should have been possible to introduce a graduated system of limited-duration subsidies for going concerns, to cushion more fully the effect of millions losing their jobs at a stroke. The material and psychological costs of sudden mass unemployment are likely to damage the social fabric more than temporary state subsidies in the interest of a less abrupt transition to a market economy.

Ten years of putting the East back on its feet and rebuilding it will cost a great deal more than the DM753 billion alleged reparation debts (plus interest) calculated by a pro-communist author in the West at the time of the *Wende*. Yet no balance can be struck between the numerous subjective injuries, based as they are on a tangled web of facts, resentment, accusations and counter-accusations, and the staggering sum of c.DM 900 billion which had poured from west to east in one form or another by 1996. But people in both east and west have taken to sneer-ing at the 'new Wall' in the heads and hearts of the Germans.

Internal disorientation

Nor is the political class doing any better: the argument over whether Bonn or Berlin should be the federal capital caused a lot of needless strife. Since there were good and bad arguments for and against either as sole capital, for once common sense suggested a solution which fits into the traditions of German federalism: Berlin as seat of government, Bonn as administrative capital with (by way of compensation) scien-tific, educational and cultural functions to come as Europe unites.

This pragmatic solution may be costly, both directly and in terms of bureaucracy, but politically and psychologically it is the right one. After forty years of paying lip-service to 'Berlin, former capital of the Reich', an either-or decision in favour of Bonn would have been a slap in the face for former citizens of the GDR. Dividing the functions of govern-ment between Berlin and Bonn should also help to cushion what could have been a one-sided shift of emphasis eastward to the new seat of government, while Bonn as administrative capital is better located to maintain links with the West. Conversely, the highest organs of the state are moving to a new federal capital where some 40 per cent of the votes in its eastern half were for the PDS.

The contortions that both government and opposition went through over essential tax increases were painful to behold, for the SPD was in a position to vote down the government's tax package in the Upper House. In government, the SPD would presumably also have increased VAT to the European level now proposed by the Kohl government. On the other hand, the decision to raise the VAT level to 15 per cent was one the federal government had taken in conjunction with the EC itself, though domestically it put the blame on Brussels.

The West German unions were still making massive wage claims (10.5%) in 1992, regardless of the economic reality in Germany of a shrinking industrial base, or of their colleagues in the East who as a result would have to wait even longer for the essential medium-term adjustment of their wages and salaries to western levels. They should instead have aimed at a more rapid income alignment between West and East through more moderate compensation for increased rates of infla-tion in the West and a supplement some 50% higher for colleagues in the East (e.g. 5% in the West, 7.5% in the East). In the meantime, as long-term unemployment rises, the unions have become more subdued and have even begun to forgo pay rises in return for job security.

Student intake in universities and colleges is rising constantly: for the first time there are more students than apprentices and trainees. It is not only additional wage costs and benefits which could bring Germany to a standstill as an industrial nation, but also the fact that its young people are striving for higher things and turning to academic learning as a path to self-fulfilment, with a corresponding drop in standards in schools and universities. In a nation of graduates, skilled trades and factory jobs are delegated to foreigners, who have already been doing the 'dirty' jobs for decades. The progressive 'nation of poets and thinkers' has been constructing a new race and class structure – white collars for the Germans, blue for the foreign sub-proletariat, with the prospect of their being able to join the progressive master race through upward assimilation in future generations.

There are other necessary reforms over which a united Germany was dragging its heels: an absolute ban on drinking and driving, speed limits for cars on autobahns and ordinary roads (both of which the ex-GDR had), interest earnings taxed at source (successfully implemented already in the USA and Denmark), laws against the laundering of drug money in Germany, tougher measures against drug trafficking, the punishment of drug pushers and, if they are foreigners, their immediate deportation, measures against organized crime and foreign mafias. Once again, false economies are being made: instead of increasing the resources of the police and equipping them properly, a fear of being accused of resorting to the police-state methods of the Third Reich seems to be paralysing any such initiative, like an insidious poison.

Regarding the difficult issue of immigrants and refugees, government and opposition have made demagogic accusations at each other, over who is responsible for the xenophobic riots against those seeking asylum, and for localized increases in the strength of the extreme right. In particular, anti-anticommunism, since 1989/91 no longer fashionable as a fundamentalist form of antifascism, has returned in the guise of a shrill antiracism, its adherents indiscriminately evoking the image of the 'ugly German' once more, but naturally excluding themselves as the only good Germans applauding Goldhagen's book, for instance.

Politicians should take a pragmatic approach to the problem. Europe, and especially Germany, is the epitome of affluence, attracting immigrants from poorer countries, particularly those recently plunged into chaos. However, massive emigration is no solution for the problems of the former 'Second World' or the declining 'Third World', the less so since those who come are often the most active and could more profitably invest their energies in their own countries. Once a certain threshold has been crossed (though it is difficult to say exactly when that occurs in individual cases), any society, however liberal and democratic its structure, will react with hostility to foreigners – mostly on the part of the lower classes for whom poor immigrants are indeed social rivals and competitors for housing and jobs. The potential for social protest in the wretched concrete blocks built in the 1960s and 1970s suddenly and almost automatically turns into xenophobia and brutal attacks on foreigners, mostly those who look non-European – from Hoyer-swerda in 1991 to Lübeck in 1996. The compromise on asylum-seekers reached in 1993 may have cooled down feelings somewhat, but each arson attack like that in Lübeck in 1996 puts people at each other's throats again.

Yet there is no parallel with 1933: government, public opinion and the population are all overwhelmingly against the cowardly, racist arson attacks. But the very attempt to explain them sociologically *as well* – by reference to the individual frustration of, in the main, socially *déclassé*, unemployed adolescents from fringe group milieus – is itself taken as proof of racist sympathies. Of course such fringe groups are misused by demagogues on the extreme Right for their own purposes. But to make society as a whole responsible for this is to indulge in the 'self-fulfilling prophecies' of the extreme Right. It would be more sensible to improve the lot of these disadvantaged fringe groups through constructive employment, social and youth policies, as a means of cutting them off from demagogues and activists on the extreme Right if at all possible.

A more nuanced definition of 'immigration' would also be useful. The Federal Republic of Germany is not a country with a tradition of immigration – unlike America, especially the USA and Canada, or Australia, or (in a very different setting) Israel, where the inhabitants of, typically, a very sparsely populated country consist almost entirely of immigrants from overseas. For some time, however, Germany has been a country to which immigrants have come to join an indigenous popula-tion which has existed for centuries. Faced with what has long been the lowest birth rate in the world, Germany is now dependent on immigra-tion (together with subsequent upward assimilation) for physical regeneration.

A compromise must be found somewhere in the middle between sui-cidally excluding the whole of the outside world, and the no less suicidal 'open door' policy advocated by the extreme 'antiracist' Left, and for a long time also by the left wing of the SPD and by the Greens. But an immigration policy is not racism; other European countries such as Great Britain and the Scandinavian countries have long been much more rigorous in controlling immigration. No one can lay claim to the only true solution to this difficult problem. Round-table talks of all concerned, native Germans and immigrants, as many as possible and on as many levels as possible, might help produce constructive solutions. These will inevitably be as diverse and as complex as the situation itself. It cannot work without compromise on all sides.

In addition, many Germans are working themselves up into an anti-*Stasi* hysteria which will undo all rational efforts to come to terms with the unpleasant GDR past. If the Third Reich was the first disaster in recent German history (Eberhard Jäckel) and the GDR the second (*Der Spiegel*), an even more catastrophic disaster now threatens to engulf Germany as both totalitarian 'pasts which will not go away' collide. While SED veterans, erstwhile practitioners of power, cleverly buy their way into the market economy as specialists of one kind or another, with or without the help of the old-boy network pulling strings, it is mostly the little people of the ex-GDR who are having to shoulder the burden of unification, both economically and psychologically.

Over-zealous attempts to get to the heart of the *Stasi* labyrinth and unravel its secrets once and for all could actually result in paralysis, especially since *Stasi* agents who are operating underground appear to be still waging war against their own people by other means – hawking their erstwhile sovereign knowledge in tasty morsels to the gutter press. The irony of the situation is that in an open democratic state under the rule of law, the credibility rating of those who were once full-time employees or even top officers in the *Stasi* appears to be higher than that of unofficial collaborators, whether real or alleged, and irrespective of how they fell into the clutches of the *Stasi*. In retrospect, the SPD's initial overzealous denunciation gives the impression of trying to divert attention from past mistakes – the actual appeasement of ruling communism from a position of safety in the West. Accordingly, a national tendency for self-flagellation has developed rapidly since unification. A nation that spent decades groaning under its division now wallows in unification as in a shared valley of tears – nor is the end yet in sight.

Where it was only natural to meet requests from the global community (UN) or relevant parts of it (NATO, EU) for the peacemaking or peacekeeping contributions of a united Germany to include a military role as well, it was self-destructive to vilify this readiness as a 'militarization of German foreign policy' in the way the SPD had done for years and one wing of the Greens still does. A united Germany simply cannot shirk such responsibilities, which would be under multinational or UN auspices. Pacifists and antimilitarists of the fundamentalist German variety are drawing the wrong lessons from the history of Germany as a power centre, literally trying to shun responsibility by turning their back on the world's ills, supposedly in the name of a higher principle. It would be altogether different if the Germans were once again embarking on risky initiatives on their own national account, but there can be no objection to contributions to multinational and international bodies at the request of the rest of the world.

Renewed instability: the PDS factor and Maastricht

Since the German edition of this book appeared in 1992, there has been a visible increase in internal political instability. This may be attributed to two principal factors: the PDS and Maastricht, though their influence is not confined to this. All other factors already mentioned are connected with it, directly (SPD, Greens, 'antiracists'; nostalgia for the GDR) or indirectly (weakness of the FDP, and of the Greens/Alliance '90 in the East) together with the reshaping of German society for Maastricht.

In general, the PDS is benefiting from the astonishing renaissance of post-communist forces in all post-communist countries, because too many voters (as in the Weimar Republic) hold the forces of democracy responsible for the post-communist mess, even though it was really caused by the communists and their renamed or reconstituted successors. The post-communist renaissance is itself evidence of how gentle and civilized the fall of communist totalitarianism was, more so than that of any other system in world history. Complaints about discrimination or 'exclusion' (PDS) of (post-)communists are pure hypocrisy: when the communists originally seized power – unlike those who replaced them in 1989/91 – they did not treat their 'enemies' with kid gloves. On the other hand, there is no point complaining about this issue, when the short memories of voters are so easily manipulated. That's life. The (post-)communists' comeback has in any case been made easier by the non-communists' mistakes.

Some misguided post-*Wende* developments of relevance specifically to the German case have already been mentioned; they provide ample explanation of how the PDS could become the focal point for repairs to damaged 'GDR biographies'. In addition, the PDS has been given a lift by the absence of genuine and public self-criticism on the part of many on the Left, in particular the SPD and those close to Jürgen Habermas during the *Historikerstreit*: Habermas and his comrades-in-arms, after letting some time pass for the sake of decency, sneaked into the 'antitotalitarian consensus' camp, as if they themselves had never denounced use of the totalitarian paradigm as a right-wing conservative or even neo-Nazi tactic. Today, they use such expressions as 'the Soviet Empire' to describe the Soviet Union, and equate the communist and Nazi systems, even though they did just the opposite during the *Historikerstreit* in 1986 – denouncing as inadmissible any criticism of communism, let alone comparison with the right-wing totalitarianism of the Nazi regime. Still avoiding all self-criticism, Habermas and his followers continue to set the tone in the main liberal press, which itself refuses to carry any serious criticism of them.

The SPD's attitude to the PDS fluctuated wildly after the *Wende*: initially it had excessively harsh words for the PDS, to cover up its previous camaraderie with the ruling SED, even when the PDS entered the *Bundestag* as a parliamentary party at the end of 1990. After the PDS had not only established itself, but was actually continuing to grow in the east, the SPD leadership appears to have realized this was a possible way for it to procure a majority. The 'Magdeburg model' operating in Sachsen-Anhalt since 1994 and quite capable of imitation in one form or another in one or more of the new *Bundesländer*, is a classical French-style 'popular front' (1936–39): a coalition of social democrats/socialists (1936: SFIO; 1994: SPD) and left-wing liberals (1936: radical socialists; 1994: Alliance '90/Greens) as a minority government tolerated by the communists in parliament (1936: PCF; 1994: PDS).

After its manifold fluctuations and contradictory stances, it is likely that the SPD might impose the 'Magdeburg model' at federal level as soon as it is in a position to do so. Such a gamble would make the situation extremely volatile, with unforeseeable consequences. In keeping with earlier developments prior to the fall of the SED-GDR, a new version of the 'Magdeburg model', or even a proper coalition with the PDS as the next logical step, would be a continuation by different means of the SPD's appeasement of the Soviet Union and the SED from *c.*1975 onwards. Nor could a government of SPD and Alliance '90/Greens, with or without PDS toleration, be justified on the grounds that the PDS must no longer be 'excluded' (*ausgegrenzt*). Automatic participation in government, whether direct (coalition) or indirect (toleration), is not the only alternative to 'exclusion', especially since the ending of PDS 'exclusion' might well mean the real exclusion of what would still probably be the strongest party, the CDU/CSU. In any case, government in opposition to the strongest party has never lasted for any length of time.

On the other hand, it is essential for Germany's political well-being that the SED's successor should be in the *Bundestag*, if only to make it absolutely clear where it stands on fundamental issues, one way or the other. To achieve this, a lowering of the blocking clause threshold (whereby a party needs at least 5 per cent of the vote to enter parliament) would have been advisable. But the most appropriate starting point for discovering the PDS's true political colours does not appear to have been tried yet, or at least has not been heard in public – the 64,000 dollar question: What's your position on the GDR?

From all that we now know, and have known since the *Wende* of 1989 at the latest, the GDR was a (left-wing) totalitarian regime, and a criminal one at that – from the beginning. At least 60,000 Germans died in GDR prisons and concentration camps, and hundreds of thousands of GDR lives were ruined in one way or another by the SED regime: these, and numerous other *Stasi* 'measures', should ensure that continuing arguments about the criminal character of the GDR regime and the SED leadership are superfluous. It goes without saying that the distinction holds good, as in other comparable cases (National Socialism, fascism), between the GDR regime and the people – in so far as they merely allowed decisions to be taken for them and things to be done to them.

So far, the PDS has refused to dissociate itself entirely from the totalitarian GDR system and its ruling party. In 1989/90, the PDS evaded dissolution of the SED and refoundation mainly because it was worried about SED party assets. But apart from erstwhile KPD assets, which were returned, SED assets had been largely accumulated by totalitarian, criminal means. Since then, the PDS has defended its erstwhile SED assets, hiding them from democratic public and governmental access – once again by criminal methods. It is only the outer trappings which have changed, through adaptation to the altered situation. But the PDS is offended if someone decribes the GDR and SED as totalitarian, and reacts even more angrily at any comparison with the Nazi dictatorship, though here, too, their erstwhile apologists in the *Historikerstreit* have long since left them in the lurch. As long as the PDS fails to dissociate itself unambiguously and publicly – at least retrospectively – from the totalitarian and criminal character of the GDR and SED, it will (rightly) be suspected of being capable of lapsing into their bad old ways at the next opportunity.

Given the strength of the PDS at local and grass-roots level, their participation in local government, if only for practical reasons, cannot be blocked. But even after distancing itself from its past there should be no question of PDS participation in government at *Land* level, let alone at federal level, under whatever guise. It would be best for all concerned to spend a probationary period in opposition. Post-communist governments in ex-communist countries, soon no doubt in 'democratic' Russia too, are bad enough. But the (direct or indirect) participation in power of an unreconstructed PDS at federal level in an expanded Germany, three-quarters of which has always been western – through the good offices of the SPD, to boot, and of an ex-civil rights party from the ex-GDR – that would be some way for a united Germany to thank the West for all its assistance since 1945! No one in a position of responsibility in the democratic parties – SPD and Alliance '90/Greens – could actually accept responsibility for the explosive repercussions. The greatest responsibility for this new instability rests with the SPD as the largest of the opposition parties pressing for participation in government by an unreconstructed PDS, the very idea of which is playing with (PDS) fire.

A further factor, no less serious and for the moment independent of the PDS, is the tendency in all industrialized countries to consolidate the economy by pruning public spending at the expense of the lower classes, while those who control the political economy continue to line their own pockets quite shamelessly. Here the Maastricht syndrome comes in: the economic crisis in the wake of German unification is only intensifying the present urge for self-destruction. The self-corruption of the political and economic classes by outrageously high salaries, pensions and golden handshakes while German millionaires are studiously evading taxation, is destroying all confidence, indispensable for any democracy, in the leading classes of parliamentary democracy. *Politikverdrossenheit* is only the beginning of that loss of confidence. And Chancellor Kohl, who may not survive politically very much longer, seems to be bent on meeting at any cost the demanding fiscal criteria for European monetary union which he himself increased by his ambition to solve Germany's financial problems. This will be at the expense of the lower classes and to the advantage of our poor millionaires and milliardaires, who, however, decide the fate of the workers, the unemployed and all those living on social welfare. With his towering figure, Kohl is also crushing all prospective successors. While his tiny majority in parliament is under fierce external and internal pressures, no real political alternative is in sight, due to the divided and confused state of mind of the Left – SPD, PDS, Greens, whose narrow majority would be no less in complete disarray and which would only lead to another set of political disasters.

History has taught us that this growing imbalance leads to social upheaval – demonstrated by recent unrest in France. It is the PDS, with its oppositional socialist-cum-communist fundamentalism, which will exploit the situation most ruthlessly and demagogically to its own ends, even though it is hardly in a position to criticize, as far as dishonest self-enrichment goes. Trouble in Germany is already gathering steam. As long as the politico-economic class makes no visible and substantial contribution to the necessary economies, Germany too can expect greater instability or even domestic social conflict.

GERMANY'S POSITION IN EUROPE

The mistrusted giant

However the Germans may twist and turn in their internal unification, they cannot escape externally from their chronic dilemma in the middle of Europe: if they are unable as a nation to surmount their most difficult crisis since 1945 constructively, they are in real trouble. Internal instability would divert their economic potential away from the reconstruction of eastern Europe, and could make their foreign policy unpredictable. Alternatively, if they survive the drastic cure of unification achieved through a measure of consolidation, then in the eyes of the world they would again be what their present Chancellor, like the first Imperial Chancellor, Bismarck, already so obviously embodies – a European giant who could upset the new balance laboriously constructed since 1945. No sooner had the contentious issue of German unification been put on the agenda than old fears began to resurface among her neighbours, especially the smaller countries, but also in France and Britain. Unification once more demonstrated the full force of the historical process, which in the end came to resemble an act of charity on Europe's part towards the Germans of the GDR. It would have been impossible – first physically, then politically – to prevent the mass exodus of GDR citizens from the disintegrating Eastern bloc, without the West itself using force.

Since 1990, as in 1871, German unification has indeed destroyed the European balance of power, especially as the collapse of the Soviet Union and Yugoslavia has eliminated useful counterbalances to a powerful Germany. One of the problems facing the new Europe after German unification will be just that – to construct a new framework for Europe, strong and flexible enough to accommodate the new Germany without her dominating the new Europe. The fact that Germany directly borders on the ex-communist East makes this no easier: aid, in whatever form, can be most effectively organized from Germany.

Here, too, the fundamental dilemma of the Germans when united – their position straddling the west–east and north–south gradients of difference in culture and affluence – has inexorably caught up with them again. From the crest of European affluence, the Rhine-Rhône-Po axis, prosperity falls the further east you go, north of the Alps, each descending step marked by a river: Elbe – Oder – Vistula – Bug – Dnieper –

Volga. It is little consolation that there is a comparable falling away of prosperity as one goes west from the Rhine: through France to Spain and Portugal in the south-west, through England to Ireland and Scotland in the north-west. This is without even considering the general north-south gradient, continuing beyond Europe into black Africa, which has become one of Europe's global problems.

However, the diminution in prosperity as one goes east, so eloquently and justifiably decried by the new citizens of Europe in the post-communist east, is a phenomenon some 2,000 years old, stretching back to the Roman conquests in Gaul under Caesar and the *limes* on the Rhine. Europe's long-term structural cleavages won't be easy to get rid of. On the other hand, shielding the EU market by cutting it off from the post-communist states in the East would contradict the fine sentiments expressed after they liberated themselves from communism. Association with these states in the near future, followed by their admission into the EU as soon as possible, could help them overcome the economic and social problems which followed the fall of communism.

Here, another dilemma is plaguing the Germans: if they refuse, for whatever reason, to help with the necessary economic recovery of the ex-communist countries in the East, there would be every justification for condemning German egoism. If they do invest, however, as they are already doing in eastern Germany and eastern Europe, they are accused of economic imperialism or colonialism. The only solution to the dilemma of how the Germans should handle the reconstruction of eastern Europe is to europeanize it, in a double sense. The more Germany becomes truly and irrevocably integrated within Europe, but equally the more non-German (and non-European) powers aid, invest and build in the liberated east and south-east of Europe, the less justification there would be for suspecting that Germany wanted to cultivate subservient client states on new 'colonial territory' in order to achieve political hegemony over Europe.

A nightmare of its own is the possibility of the GDR syndrome recurring in former pre-1937 or even pre-1914 German territories in the East, as is indeed already happening in the area of East Prussia around Königsberg/Kaliningrad, which was Soviet after 1945. There, non-Germans remember their region's German cultural traditions, speak German and claim they should again be part of Germany, or at least within the realm of the DM. That is why the Germans should take their neighbours' fears seriously: power has always fed an increased will to power. The future of Germany and Europe depends on whether the Germans can break this historical mechanism.

Another catastrophe would be for an Austria led by Jörg Haider – as is now conceivable – to come knocking on the door seeking admission to some new *Anschluß*. Even the smallest version of *Großdeutschland* would be anathema to Europe and would fatally overstrain the principle of 'national self-determination'. Situated in the middle of Europe, the Germans must finally recognize that they are the capstone in the infinitely complex and delicate arched vault of the architecture of Europe. Even their partial unification since 1990 makes the capstone itself too heavy for Europe, again as in 1871 and 1938. Only when Germany was divided was the capstone able to function properly, neutralizing and balancing Europe's internal tensions. Any further increase in its size would bring down the whole architecture of Europe, once again. But equally, the capstone must not be allowed to crumble, for it would then be unable to hold together the architecture of Europe. Finding and maintaining the right proportions and consistency for the European capstone is an exacting balancing act between many complex internal and external factors, demanding the utmost caution, tact and sensitivity, especially towards Europe.

As Germany tries to find its proper place in the world, the federal government has been vacillating between unnecessary shows of strength and acts of irresponsible foreign policy: it was not fitting for a German government to be the first to express its desire for German Permanent Membership of the UN Security Council. If, on account of the powerful position it actually occupies, Germany had been offered it by the world, then – once again – it could not have refused. But for its own Foreign Minister to request it openly, in a most undiplomatic rant, moreover, is merely a further act of folly and evidence of a lack of sensitivity in high places. The permanent recognition of Croatia by Germany without previous binding guarantees for the Krajina Serbs (autonomy) is also turning out to be a handicap for any peaceful German foreign policy.

Outlook: Germany a superpower in the making?

Behind the backs of the initially jubilant Germans, there are factors at work which point towards future division and which confront the united Germany with a new dilemma. The new German Question, addressed both to the Germans and to the outside world, is accordingly now: if they create inner unity, more or less, perhaps ten years after unification in 1990, i.e. around the turn of the century, then the threat – not for reasons of intrinsic evil or stupidity on the part of the Germans, but in accordance with universal historical mechanisms – is that Germany, its status as economic giant consolidated, will again flex its economic muscle if its integration within Europe proves not to be permanent. If the united Germans abandon themselves completely to the dynamics of internal confusion as created by the fusion of two so contrary systems, chaos threatens within, and unpredictability without. The most recent version of the German Question can also be summarized thus: after fluctuating for more than 1,000 years between unity and division, can the Germans now finally succeed in constructively blending internal national unity and peaceful external exercise of their enormous power?

It will always be difficult to find a solution which satisfies everyone, for the dividing line between unity and the threat of hegemony, between internal instability and external paralysis, is a narrow one. The ideal solution – a domestically stable, democratic Germany without hegemonic tendencies in Europe – would be too good to become true, judging by all historical and political precedents. Nevertheless, this is the goal on which all effort should focus.

When the present generation of politicians like Kohl and Genscher, for whom the German catastrophe of 1945 is a living memory, leaves the stage, there is no guarantee that subsequent generations will remain as likeably modest as the Germans were advised to be after 1945. So, about a decade on from unification will probably be the moment of truth for Germany and Europe, if the Germans manage the transition to internal unity after all. The next major economic crisis after that will show whether internal democracy and external integration within Europe have become sufficiently strong for Germany to take coming problems in its stride. The Germans would have to remain ready to combine their legitimate national interests with those of Europe, and to subordinate national to European interests. If, one day, after successfully achieving internal unity, they were to demand a power-political role to match their paramount economic position, the consequences for Europe would be catastrophic. In domestic terms, the containment necessary for maximum defusing of political power is provided by parliamentary democracy and federalism; externally, German energies can be best harnessed by effective and irrevocable integration within Europe.

All democrats interested in a peaceful future for Germany and Europe should use the next critical decade working towards the right permanent structures in Germany and Europe, but also helping to educate the united Germans politically by rational analysis of history – both German and European history. This includes distinguishing between the historical-political categories of *Reich* and *Nation*. For the Germans, the foundation or refounding of a 'Reich' has always included a claim to German hegemony in Europe, a claim which is incompatible with the pluralistic architecture of our continent. Instead, the Germans must learn to see themselves as a member of the Latin family of nations, whose original impulse towards self-organization from below, based on equal rights, eventually became after more than a thousand years the success story (so far) of democracy and human rights. The Germans have a legitimate place in such a Europe, and given their central geographical position as the capstone of Europe, even a central place. Only they must never again succumb to the temptation of wanting to lord it over Europe.

Meanwhile, the ever-daunting German Question in its most recent guise may yet take a dramatic turn, for quite unexpected reasons. With the triumph of the contraceptive pill even before the symbolic year 1968, Germany, both divided *and* united, has been enjoying (if that is the right word) the lowest birth-rate in the world. Most young Germans are shunning the trouble of bearing and rearing children. Instead, the German economy is having to rely on importing sufficient numbers of able-bodied young immigrants to secure the labour and dues vital to uphold social security for ageing, childless Germans.

Germany's impending demographic collapse could, at least, solve one quantitative dimension of the perennial German Question referred to by a despairing Clemenceau at Versailles in 1919. Qualitative decline of the German industrial landscape would follow inexorably, under the pressure of the rapidly modernizing world markets. The social cohesion between the generations must inevitably break down if there are too many old-aged people left, the young ones do not find enough jobs and they, in their turn, refuse to conceive the next generation in sufficient numbers. Under the pressure of the ambivalent consequences of German unification, Europeanization embodied by Maastricht, and economic globalization, Germany is now rent by manifold internal contradictions, e.g. between East and West Germans, between xenophobic outrages and rabid anti-racism, right-wing extremists and fundamentalist 'anti-facism', while all dissent is taunted as 'racism', 'anti-Semitism', 'neo-facism' or indeed, 'nationalism'. Thus Germany, unhappily united and polarized, is already in the midst of heavy 'weather'.[2] On the other hand, new arrivals from many quarters of the globe will adapt to their new haven of (relative) prosperity, and universalize the German Question by behaving, in the middle of Europe – as Germans.

Chronological table

1806   Confederation of the Rhine (to 1813): end of (first) German Reich (since 962). Austrian Empire (since 1804). Defeat of Prussia at Jena and Auerstedt: collapse of old Prussia. Germany remains a power vacuum (to 1871).

1807   Peace of Tilsit: territorially diminished Prussia preserved as vassal state of Napoleon I; Duchy of Warsaw as French client state (to 1813).

1808   Prussian reforms as response to French Revolution and defeat of Prussia.

1813   Wars of Liberation (to 1815): defeat of France by European Grand Coalition.

1815   Congress of Vienna: reorganization of Europe. German Confederation; Rhineland to Prussia: polarization between agrarian land east of the Elbe ('Ostelbien') and industrializing west ('Westelbien').

1830   July Revolution in France, unrest in Germany too.

1834   German *Zollverein*: customs union under Prussian leadership, without Austria.

1848   Revolution in Europe, including Germany (to 1849): Paulskirche Assembly in Frankfurt am Main: *großdeutsch* or *kleindeutsch*? i.e. Greater Germany (with Austria) or Lesser Germany (without Austria, under Prussian leadership)? First German-Danish War.

1849   Paulskirche Constitution: *kleindeutsch* option, King of Prussia as Emperor of German Reich; constitutional monarchy, rejected by Prussia under pressure from Russia. Constitution for Prussia; Schwarzenberg's Plan for *Mitteleuropa* – 'Empire of the 70 millions'.

1850   Erfurt Union parliament; Olmütz Proclamation: Prussia withdraws under pressure from Russia.
Industrial take-off in Germany.

1856	End of Crimean War (since 1853/54): Britain and Russia withdraw from Continent: relative power vacuum in Europe: France isolated *vis-à-vis* the German Question.
1858	Wilhelm Prince Regent in Prussia: liberal 'New Era'; Prussia aims for 'moral conquests' in Germany.
1859	Italian Risorgimento; victory of Italian national movement influences German national movement.
1861	Prussian army reform, constitutional conflict and threat of revolution.
1862	Bismarck Prussian prime minister (to 1890).
1864	Second German–Danish War: Prussia and Austria defeat Denmark.
1866	German War: victory of Prussia over Austria at Königgrätz; Prussian hegemony in Germany.
1867	North German Federation (to 1871) with modified 1849 constitution. *Ausgleich* or 'Compromise': Dual Monarchy Austria–Hungary (to 1918), orientated towards the Balkans.
1870	South German Hohenzollern candidature for Spanish throne; Franco-Prussian War (to 1871): German victory over France.
1871	Foundation of the Reich: Second German Empire (to 1918): Germany as power centre, 1871–1945. German Reich as federal state: King of Prussia–German Kaiser; constitutional monarchy with modified 1849/67 constitution; *Kulturkampf* against Catholics (to 1887); boom years of rapid industrial expansion.
1873	World economic crisis, also in Germany (and Austria).
1878	Congress of Berlin: Bismarck as Europe's arbitrator. Anti-socialist law (to 1890): struggle against social democracy. First appearance in public of German anti-Semitism.
1879	Dual Alliance of Germany with Austria-Hungary (to 1918). Protective tariffs for agriculture (against Russia) and industry (against Great Britain).
1882	Dual Alliance expanded to Triple Alliance with entry of Italy (to 1914).
1884	Colonial politics: German protectorates in Togo, the Cameroons, German South-West Africa, German East Africa, and in the Pacific.
1888	Year of the Three Emperors: death of Wilhelm I and Frederick III; Wilhelm II Kaiser (to 1918).
1890	Fall of Bismarck: Caprivi Chancellor of the Reich (to 1894);

Mitteleuropa as alternative to subsequent *Weltpolitik*; 'New Course' – liberal domestic politics.

1894	Hohenlohe Chancellor (to 1900): transition to *Weltpolitik*.
1898	Construction of German battle fleet.
1900	Bülow Chancellor (to 1909): *Weltpolitik* – 'a place in the sun' for Germany.
1905	First Morocco crisis. Schlieffen Plan for war on two fronts, first against France, then against Russia.
1908/09	Bosnian annexation crisis.
1909	Bethmann Hollweg Chancellor (to 1917): aims at reconciliation at home (with SPD) and abroad (with Britain).
1911	Second Morocco crisis. For first time strong influence of Pan-Germans on German foreign policy.
1914	First World War (to 1918): after initial German victories in the west, defeat on the Marne; positional warfare; victories against Russians in East Prussia; war aims: 'bid for world power'.
1916	Supreme Army Command under Hindenburg and Ludendorff (to 1918): effectively a military dictatorship.
1917	Fall of Bethmann Hollweg; *Reichstag* peace resolution. Unrestricted submarine warfare; USA enters war. SPD – USPD (Independent Socialists) split. Russian Revolutions in February/March and October/November.
1918	Military defeat of Germany; November Revolution; monarchy overthrown; founding of (communist) KPD. Request by Austria and German Bohemia for *Anschluß* rejected by Allies.
1919	Spartacus uprising; Weimar National Assembly: 'Weimar Coalition': (SPD, Centre, Democrats); Friedrich Ebert President of the Reich (to 1925); Weimar constitution. Treaty of Versailles: territorial losses, military restrictions, reparations, 'war guilt'. Ban on *Anschluß*: Austria independent state against her will.
1920	Kapp *putsch*; first *Reichstag* elections: Weimar coalition loses majority; split in USPD; KPD gains; founding of NSDAP (National Socialist German Workers' Party). Westward advance of Red Army halted at Warsaw; no march on Berlin.
1922	Treaty of Rapallo between Germany and Soviet Russia: cooperation against Poland.

1923   Inflation peaks; occupation of Ruhr and fighting; serious domestic crisis, Hitler *Putsch* in Munich; polarization between nationalist Bavaria and SPD/KPD governments in Saxony and Thuringia; *Rentenmark*: end of inflation.

1924   Two *Reichstag* elections (June, December); Dawes Plan: restructuring of German reparations, US loan: political consolidation of Weimar Republic; culture flourishes, especially in Berlin.

1925   Hindenburg elected President of the Reich.
Locarno Pacts: outward consolidation, Reich recognizes new frontiers, but not eastern frontiers: no 'Eastern Locarno'.

1928   Grand coalition led by SPD (to 1930).

1929   World economic crisis: devastating repercussions, in particular on Germany.

1930   Fall of last parliamentary government under Hermann Müller (SPD); authoritarian presidential cabinets under Heinrich Brüning (to 1932): emergency decrees.
Reichstag election: NSDAP wins 107 seats: SPD tolerates Brüning (to 1932).

1931   Height of world economic crisis: France prevents customs union between Germany and Austria.

1932   Six million unemployed in Germany; elections for President of the Reich: Hindenburg re-elected, beating NSDAP candidate Hitler; two *Reichstag* elections: NSDAP wins 230 (196) seats; polarization between KPD and NSDAP intensifies; civil war conditions; presidential cabinets under von Papen, Schleicher.

1933   Hitler Chancellor of the Reich (to 1945): end of Weimar Republic; 'seizure of power': totalitarian dictatorship, terror, concentration camps, rearmament, 'revision' of Versailles. Beginning of official state anti-Semitism.

1934   'Röhm Affair'; death of Hindenburg: Hitler President of the Reich.

1935   Universal conscription; return of Saarland to Reich; Nuremberg Laws against Jews.

1936   Four-Year Plan to place German economy on a war footing; occupation of Rhineland; intervention in Spanish Civil War ('Condor Legion'); Berlin–Rome axis; Anti-Comintern Pact. Olympic games in Berlin, giving a propagandist boost to Hitler's Germany.

1938   *Anschluß* with Austria: Greater German Reich; Munich

Agreement; annexation of Sudetenland; pogrom against Jews (*Reichskristallnacht*).

1939   Occupation of remaining Czech lands: Bohemia and Moravia 'Protectorate' of the Reich; re-annexation of Memelland; Hitler–Stalin Pact; Danzig crisis; Germany invades Poland: Second World War (to 1945); 'Polish campaign': Poland divided between Germany and USSR; 'Generalgouvernement' of Poland; 'Phoney War' (*Sitzkrieg*) in West.

1940   Victory over France; 'Battle of Britain': no German invasion. Italy enters war.

1941   Germans conquer Yugoslavia and Greece; Invasion of USSR. Germany declares war on USA; 'Final Solution'.

1942   After further victories up to Caucasus, Sixth Army surrounded at Stalingrad. German defeat at El Alamein.

1943   Stalingrad: turning point of war in Europe; German retreat: 'total war'.

1944   Invasion of Allies in Normandy; 20 July: failed attempt on Hitler's life.

1945   Final stages of battle for Germany and Berlin; death of Hitler. Germany as power vacuum, 1945–1990. 8 May: unconditional surrender of Greater German Reich; Allied Control Council with sovereignty extending to Oder-Neiße line; four occupation zones, four sectors in Berlin. Austria under separate Allied occupation. Potsdam Agreement: separate developments in East and West.

1946   Forced merger of KPD and SPD–SED in Soviet Occupation Zone. Cold War exacerbates division; US and British zones economically unified as Bizonia.

1948   Currency reform in the Western zones; Berlin Blockade and airlift (to 1949). Western zones included in Marshall Plan.

1949   Federal Republic and GDR (to 1990), initially autonomous. Adenauer Federal Chancellor (to 1963).

1950   Korean War: 'Korean War boom' and 'economic miracle' in Federal Republic. Adenauer offers Allies a German 'contribution to defence'.

1952   Closure of internal German border by GDR; abolition of GDR's five *Länder*, replaced by fifteen administrative districts; increased sovietization of GDR: mass exodus to Federal Republic.

1953   17 June: uprising in GDR. Great electoral victory of CDU/CSU.

1955   Federal Republic in NATO, GDR in Warsaw Pact.

1956   *Bundeswehr* – National People's Army. Uprising in Hungary, unrest in Poland.

1958   Khrushchev's Berlin ultimatum: mass exodus from GDR via West Berlin.

1961   Berlin Wall (to 1989) to halt mass exodus from GDR ('anti-fascist protective wall'). Change of tack in West Berlin: 'progress through *rapprochement*'.

1962   John F. Kennedy in West Berlin: '*Ich bin ein Berliner*'.

1963   Adenauer resigns: Ludwig Erhard Federal Chancellor (to 1966); introduction of passes for West Berliners to enter East Berlin: policy of 'little steps'.

1966   Recession in the Federal Republic: Grand Coalition CDU/CSU with SPD Kiesinger/Brandt (to 1969): consolidation of economy through 'concerted action'.

1967   2 June: start of student unrest in West Berlin and Federal Republic.

1968   Emergency laws, Easter disturbances, height of student unrest.
        GDR forces participate in invasion of Czechoslovakia by Warsaw Pact troops.

1969   Socialist–Liberal coalition SPD/FDP (to 1982) Brandt/Scheel (to 1974): reforms, general internal amnesty, new external *Ostpolitik*.

1970   Moscow Treaty, Warsaw Treaty: *modus vivendi* with communist East.

1971   Walter Ulbricht resigns: Erich Honecker General Secretary of Central Committee of SED (to 1989).

1972   Electoral victory of SPD – strongest party in *Bundestag* for first time. Basic Treaty Federal Republic–GDR: GDR recognized; both German states in United Nations; increased emphasis on divergent identity of GDR (*Abgrenzung*).

1973   World economic crisis, initially with little impact on Federal Republic.

1974   Guillaume Affair: Willy Brandt resigns; Helmut Schmidt Federal Chancellor (to 1982).

1976   Incipient crisis in Federal Republic: unemployment increases: CDU/CSU again strongest party in *Bundestag* election.

1979   War in Afghanistan; crisis within USSR.

1980   Setback for SPD in *Bundestag* election: Socialist–Liberal coalition weakened.

1981   State of war in Poland: Erich Honecker (SED) and Helmut Schmidt (SPD) for stability in People's Republic of Poland.

1982   Missiles crisis. *Wende* in Federal Republic: coalition of CDU/CSU and FDP under Helmut Kohl.

1983   *Bundestag* election: CDU/CSU–FDP coalition confirmed. Massive loans from West postpone bankruptcy of GDR.

1985   Gorbachev General Secretary of CPSU (to 1991): attempted reform through *perestroika* and *glasnost*; death throes of USSR, internal crisis in GDR intensifies.

1987   Honecker's state visit to Federal Republic. Joint SPD–SED paper.

1989   Hungary opens its border to west: mass exodus from GDR; *Wende* in GDR: fall of Honecker; transitional government under Hans Modrow (SED); opening of Berlin Wall.

1990   18 March: first free election to *Volkskammer*: victory of CDU-East; GDR 'wound up': USSR agrees to unity.
3 October: unification of both German states up to Oder–Neiße line; first all-German *Bundestag* elections: victory of CDU/CSU and FDP.

1991   Moscow *putsch*: end of USSR. General malaise in united Germany; 'Wall in people's heads'; unemployment and 'dismantling' in East.

1992   Opening of *Stasi* files intensifies internal crisis: smear campaign and suicides; strikes in West; Republican and DVU gains in *Landtag* elections, party crises.

1994   CDU/CSU scrapes home in *Bundestag* election with a slender majority. Pruning of welfare system; unemployment reaches post-war height.

1996   Chancellor Kohl surpasses Adenauer in holding office. Financial chaos; further axing of social security, and growing mass unemployment; 4.7 million unemployed.

Notes

PREFACE

1 Geiss, I. (1993) *Europa – Vielfalt und Einheit. Eine historische Erklärung*, Mannheim: Meyers Forum 12.
2 For the best, most recent and most rational overview by a German historian, see Schulze, H. (1996) *Kleine deutsche Geschichte*, Munich: C.H. Beck.

INTRODUCTION

1 Bibio, I. (1991) *Die deutsche Hysterie. Ursachen und Geschichte*, Frankfurt am Main: verlag neue kritik.
2 Fischer, F. (1967) *Germany's Aims in the First World War*, London: Chatto & Windus.
3 *Ibid.*, (1993), *Forever in the Shadow of Hitler. The Dispute About the Germans' Understanding of History. Original Documents of the 'Historikerstreit', the Controversy Concerning the Singularity of the Holocaust*, Atlantic Highlands, N.J.
4 Geiss, I. (1996) 'Gegenwart als Geschichte oder Geschichte der Gegenwart. Ein kritischer Doppel-Essay', in: *Historische Mitteilungen der Ranke-Gesellschaft* 9(2), 283–309.
5 For this author's position, see Geiss, I. (1996) 'The Historical Position of German National Socialism: Between Communism and Fascism', in A. Bonnell *et al.* (eds) *Conscience, and Opposition. Essays in German History in Honour of John A. Moses*, New York: Peter Lang, pp. 309–28.

1 CONCEPTUAL AND EUROPEAN FRAMEWORK

1 This author's translation. See also Aristotle, *Politics*, ed, and translated by Ernest Barker, Oxford 1945, 4th impression, 1968, Book IV, ch. xii, §1, p. 185; for the reference in the following sentence, ibid., Book IV, ch. ix, §4, p. 290.
2 Geiss, I. Verfuß, K. and Wunderer, H. (1995) *Der Zerfall der Sowjetunion*, Brennpunkt Geschichte, Frankfurt am Main: Verlag Moritz Diesterweg.
3 For a detailed analysis, see Geiss, I. (1994) 'Great Powers and Empires: Historical Mechanisms of their Making and Breaking', in G. Lundestad (ed.) *The Fall of Great Powers. Peace, Stability, and Legitimacy*, Oslo,

Oxford: Scandinavian University Press, Oxford University Press, pp. 23–43.
4 Geiss, I. (1993) *Europa – Vielfalt und Einheit. Eine historische Erklärung*. Meyers Forum 12, Mannheim: Bibliographisches Institut.
5 Geiss, I. (1995) *Der Jugoslawienkrieg*, Brennpunkt Geschichte, 2nd edn with Gabriele Intemann, Frankfurt am Main: Diesterweg.
6 Geiss, I. (1993) 'Der Holzweg des deutschen Sonderwegs', *Kirchliche Zeitgeschichte* 7(2), 191–208.
7 For greater detail, see Geiss, 'Holzweg', ibid., pp. 195–197.
8 Bibio, *op. cit.* Introduction, n. 1.
9 von Beyme, K. (1991) *Hauptstadtsuche*, Frankfurt am Main: Suhrkamp, pp. 112 ff.
10 Szücs, J. (1990) *Die drei historischen Regionen Europas*, Frankfurt am Main: verlag neue kritik, p. 60.

2 FROM POWER VACUUM TO POWER CENTRE: FROM THE FIRST TO THE SECOND REICH, 1806–1871

1 Berding, H. (1971) *Herrschafts- und Gesellschaftspolitik im Königreich Westphalen, 1807–1813*, Göttingen: Vandenhoek & Ruprecht.
2 Kosellek, R. (1975) *Preußen zwischen Reform und Revolution*, 2nd edn, Stuttgart: Klett; Vogel, B. (ed.) (1980) *Preußische Reformen 1807–1820*, Neue Wissenschaftliche Bibliothek 96, Königstein/Ts: Athenäum Verlag.
3 Henning, F.–W. (1989) *Die Industrialisierung in Deutschland 1800–1914*, 2nd edn, Paderborn: Schöningh.
4 Fenske, H. (1991) 'Ungeduldige Zuschauer. Die Deutschen und die europäische Expansion 1815–1980' in W. Reinhard (ed.) *Imperialistische Kontinuität und nationale Ungeduld*, Frankfurt am Main: Fischer Taschenbuch Verlag, pp. 87–123.
5 Wollstein, G. (1977) *Das 'Großdeutschland' der Paulskirche. Nationale Ziele in der bürgerlichen Revolution 1848–9* Düsseldorf, Droste.
6 Fenske, *op. cit.* n. 4.
7 Baumgart, W. (1972) *Der Friede von Paris 1856*, Munich and Vienna: Oldenbourg; Schroeder, P.W. (1972) *Austria, Great Britain and the Crimean War*, New York: Ithaca and London, Cornell University Press.
8 Boldt, F. (1996) *Kultur versus Staatlichkeit. Zur Genesis der modernen politischen Kultur in den böhmischen Ländern im Widerspiel kultureller und politischer Bewegungen bei den böhmischen Tschechen und Deutschen bis zum Jahre 1898*, Prague: Karolinum.
9 Chastain, J. (1988) *The Liberation of Sovereign Peoples. The French Foreign Policy of 1848*, Athens, Ohio: Ohio University Press.
10 This is a special point made by Bucholz, A. (1991) *Moltke, Schlieffen and Prussian War Planning*, New York, Oxford: Berg, pp. 26–28.

3 GERMANY AS A POWER CENTRE: SECOND AND THIRD REICHS 1871–1945

1 Thus Mommsen, W.J. (1990) *Der autoritäre Nationalstaat. Verfassung, Gesellschaft und Kultur im deutschen Kaiserreich*, Frankfurt am Main: Fischer Taschenbuchverlag.

2 Hobsbawm, E. (1987) *The Age of Empire 1875–1914*, London: Weidenfeld & Nicolson, ch. 10. 'The Career open to Talent', pp. 186–200; Nipperdey, T. (1990) *Deutsche Geschichte 1866–1918, I, Arbeitswelt und Bürgertum*, Munich: C.H. Beck, ch. XIV, 'Die Wissenschaften, pp. 602–18, 623–29; Salewski, M. (1986) *Zeitgeist und Zeitmaschine. Science Fiction und Geschichte*. Munich: dtv.

3 Kennedy, P. (1980) *The Rise of Anglo-German Antagonism 1860–1914*, London: Allen & Unwin.

4 Geiss, I. (1991) *Der lange Weg in die Katastrophe. Die Vorgeschichte des Ersten Weltkrieges 1815–1914*, 2nd edn, Munich: Piper; *ibid.*, (1976) *German Foreign Policy 1871–1914*, London: Routledge & Kegan Paul.

5 Calleo, D. (1978) *The German problem reconsidered. Germany and the world order, 1870 to the present*, Cambridge, Cambridge University Press, 1978, p. 206.

6 Kann, R.A. (1962) *The Habsburg Empire*, New York: Frederick A. Praeger.

7 Albertini, L. (1966) *The Origins of the War of 1914*, 2nd edn, London: Oxford University Press, 3 vols.

8 Weber, M. (1961) *Gesammelte Politische Schriften*, ed. J. Winkelmann, Tübingen: J.C.B. Mohr; paperback edn 1988, p. 23.

9 Chickering, R. (1984) *We Men Who feel Most German. A Cultural Study of the Pan-German League, 1866–1914*, Boston and London: George Allen & Unwin.

10 Goldhagen, D.J. (1996) *Hitler's willing Executioners*. Ordinary Germans and the Holocaust, New York: Alfred A. Knopf, ignores the comparative dimension.

11 Bendikat, E. (1988) *Wahlkämpfe in Europa 1884 bis 1889. Parteiensysteme und Politikstile in Deutschland, Frankreich und Großbritannien*, Wiesbaden: Deutscher Universitätsverlag, p. 62.

12 For the messianic element in early social democracy, see Seebacher-Brandt, B. (1988) *Bebel. Künder und Kärrner im Kaiserreich*, Berlin: J.H.W. Dietz Nachf; Hölscher, L. (1988) *Weltgericht oder Revolution. Protestantische und sozialistische Zukunftsvorstellung im deutschen Kaiserreich*, Stuttgart Klett/Cotta.

13 Fischer, F. (1967) *Germany's Aims in the First World War*, London: Chatto & Windus.

14 Hillgruber, A. (1968) 'Die "Krieg-in-Sicht-Krise" 1875 – Wegscheide der Politik der europäischen Großmächte in der späten Bismarckzeit', in E. Schulin (ed.) *Studien zur europäischen Geschichte. Gedenkschrift Martin Göhring*, Wiesbaden: Franz Steiner Verlag, pp. 239–53.

15 See the official German documents for the pre-war period, *Die Große Politik der Europäischen Kabinette 1871–1914. Sammlung der diplomatischen Akten des Auswärtigen Amtes*, ed. J. Lepsius, 39 vols, Berlin: Deutsche Verlagsgesellschaft für Politik und Geschichte, 1922–27, vol. III, nos 458, 461, 477.

16 Fischer, *op. cit.* n. 13; Geiss, I. (1990) 'The German Version of Imperialism, 1898–1914: Weltpolitik', in G. Schöllgen (ed.) *Escape into War? The Foreign Policy of Imperial Germany*, Oxford and New York: Berg, pp. 105–19. For the oldest, yet still valid, survey of imperialism in general (unfortunately covering only the period up to 1902), see Langer, W.L. (1977) *European Alliances and Alignments, 1871–1890*, reprint, Westport: Green-

wood (originally published 1938, New York: Knopf); *ibid.* (1968) *The Diplomacy of Imperialism 1890–1902*, 2nd edn, New York: Knopf.

17 Schöllgen, G. (1984) *Imperialismus und Gleichgewicht. Deutschland, England und die orientalische Frage 1871–1914*, Munich: Oldenbourg.
18 Djordjević, D. (1965) *Révolutions nationales des peuples balkaniques 1804–1914*, Belgrade; *ibid.* (1981) *The Balkan Revolutionary Tradition*, New York: Columbia University Press.
19 For details of the socio-economic dilemma created by the impact of industrial revolution on Germany, see Geiss, *German Foreign Policy, 1871–1914*, *op. cit.* n. 4, following Eckart Kehr and G.W.F. Hallgarten, pp. 13–15.
20 For a more detailed analysis, see Geiss, I. (1996) 'Deutschland und Österreich-Ungarn beim Kriegsausbruch 1914. Eine machthistorische Analyse', in M. Gehler (ed.) *Ungleiche Partner? Österreich und Deutschland in ihrer gegenseitigen Wahrnehmung. Historische Analysen und Vergleiche aus dem 19. und 20. Jahrhundert*, Stuttgart: Franz Steiner Verlag, pp. 375–95.
21 Generally, see Fischer, *German War Aims op. cit.* n. 13.
22 For details as part of German war aims, see Geiss, I. (1960) *Der polnische Grenzstreifen 1914–1918. Ein Beitrag zur deutschen Kriegszielpolitik im Ersten Weltkrieg, Historische Studien 378*, Hamburg and Lübeck; Polish edition, Warsaw 1964.
23 Riezler, K. (1972) *Tagebücher, Aufsätze, Dokumente*, ed. K.-D. Erdmann, Gottingen: Vandenhoek & Ruprecht, p. 224.
24 *Ibid.*, p. 268.
25 *Ibid.*, pp. 229, 234, 360, 368, 461, 478.
26 Wheeler-Benett, J.W. (1918) *The Forgotten Peace, March 1918*, London: Macmillan; reprinted New York: Norton, 1971.
27 Zimmermann, L. (1958) *Die Außenpolitik der Weimarer Republik*, Göttingen: Musterschmidt.
28 Höltje, C. (1958) *Die Weimarer Republik und das Ost-Locarno-Problem. 1919–1934, Revision oder Garantie der deutschen Ostgrenze von 1919*, Würzburg: Holzner.
29 Heinemann, U. (1983) *Die verdrängte Niederlage. Politische Öffentlichkeit und Kriegsschuldfrage in der Weimarer Zeit*, Göttingen: Vandenhoek & Ruprecht.

4 GERMANY AS A POWER VACUUM: DIVISION, 1945–1989/90

1 von Flocken, J. and Klonovsky, M. (1991) *Stalins Lager in Deutschland 1945–1950*, Berlin.
2 For a most recent collective study see Larres, K. and Panayi, P. (eds) (1996) *The Federal Republic of Germany since 1949. Politics, Society and Economy before and after Unification*, London: Longman, with a contribution by this author: 'The Federal Republic of Germany in International Politics Before and After Unification', pp. 137–65.
3 von Schubert, K. (1970) *Westbewaffnung und Westintegration. Die innere Auseinandersetzung um die militärische und außenpolitische Orientierung der Bundesrepublik*, Stuttgart: Deutsche Verlagsanstalt.
4 Ash, T.G. (1993) *In Europe's Name. Germany and the Divided Continent*, London: Jonathan Cape.
5 *Forever in the Shadow of Hitler? Original Documents of the Historikerstreit,*

The Controversy Concerning the Singularity of the Holocaust, Humanities Press, N.J., 1993, with two short contributions by this author, pp. 147 ff., 254–58; for more detailed assessments, yet passed over in silence by our 'New Orthodoxy', see Geiss, I. (1988) *Die Habermas-Kontroverse. Ein deutscher Streit*, Berlin: Siedler; *ibid.* (1992) *Der Hysterikerstreit. Ein unpolemischer Essay*, Bonn.
6 Aktion Sühnezeichen/Friedensdienste (1988) *Das SPD-SED-Papier. Der Streit der Ideologien und die gemeinsame Sicherheit*, Freiburg: Dreisam Verlag.
7 Zubok, V. and Pleshakov, C. (1996) *Inside the Kremlin's Cold War. From Stalin to Khrushchev*, Cambridge, Mass.: Harvard University Press, pp. 248–56.

5 UNITED GERMANY SINCE 1989/90

1 Geiss, I. (1991) 'The Trouble with German Unity', *The Australian Journal of Politics and History*, vol. 37, no. 2, pp. 236–45.
2 *Ibid.*, p. 245.

Further reading

Ardagh, J. (1995) *Germany and the Germans*, 3rd edn, London.
Berghahn, V.R. (1987) *Modern Germany. Society, Economy and Politics in the Twentieth Century*, 2nd edn, Cambridge.
Carr, W. (1991) *A History of Germany 1815–1990*, 4th edn, London.
Craig, G.A. (1981) *Germany 1866–1945*, Oxford.
Evans, R.J. (1989) *In Hitler's Shadow. West German Historians and the Attempt to Escape from the Nazi Past*, London.
—— (1987) *Rethinking German History. Nineteenth Century Germany and the Origins of the Third Reich*, London.
Fulbrook, M. (1991) *The Fontana History of Germany 1918–1990. The Divided Nation*, London.
—— (1995) *A Concise History of Germany*, Cambridge.
Hildebrand, K. (1991) *The Third Reich*, London.
Larres, K. and Panayi, P. (1996) *The Federal Republic of Germany since 1949. Politics, Society and Economy before and after Unification*, London.
Mertes, M., Muller, S. and Winkler, H.A. (eds) (1996) *In Search of Germany*, New Brunswick and London.
Taylor, A.J.P. (1956) *The Course of German History: A Survey of the Development of Germany since 1815*, London.
Turner Jr., J.A. (1992) *Germany from Partition to Reunification*, New Haven and London.

Index